HOW TO BE A MORE SUCCESSFUL LANGUAGE LEARNER:

Toward Learner Autonomy

SECOND EDITION

Joan Rubin
&
Irene Thompson

HEINLE & HEINLE PUBLISHERS
A Division of Wadsworth, Inc.
Boston, Massachusetts 02116 USA

The publication of *How to Be a More Successful Language Learner,
Second Edition* was directed by the members of the Heinle & Heinle ESL
Publishing Team:

David C. Lee, *Editorial Director*
Kristin Thalheimer, *Production Editor*

Also participating in the publication of this program were:

Publisher: Stanley J. Galek
Editorial Production Manager: Elizabeth Holthaus
Assistant Editor: Kenneth Mattsson
Project Manager: Margaret Cleveland
Manufacturing Coordinator: Mary Beth Lynch
Interior Design and Composition: Greg Johnson, Art Directions
Cover Artist: Cynthia Jabar
Cover Design: Bortman Design Group

Library of Congress Cataloging-in-Publication Data

Rubin, Joan, 1932–
    How to be a more successful language learner : toward learner autonomy /
Joan Rubin & Irene Thompson
    p. cm.
    ISBN 0-8384-4734-1
    1. Language and languages — Study and teaching.   I. Thompson, Irene.   II. Title
P51.R8   1994
418' .007 — dc20   93–42857
                                                                            CIP

Heinle and Heinle Publishers is a division of Wadsworth , Inc.

Manufactured in the United States of America

International Standard Book Number: 0-8384-4734-1

10   9   8   7   6   5   4

To our husbands

Patrick James Ryan and Richard Thompson

Contents

$\mathcal{P}$REFACE

If you are presently studying a foreign language or are planning to do so, this book is written for you. In it you will find concrete suggestions to help you become a more effective and successful language learner. You will also become acquainted with a host of techniques based on research into second language learning and on actual classroom experience that will enable you to approach the study of a foreign language in a meaningful and productive way.

In today's world, contact with speakers of languages other than English is increasingly common; we encounter such people in school, in our travels, and in our jobs. As these contacts increase, so do our need and motivation to study foreign languages. For many, the study of a foreign language is a satisfying and truly rewarding experience. Others, however, consider it a frustrating, nearly impossible undertaking. We believe that you can avoid a great deal of frustration and disappointment if you take the time to learn some basic facts about yourself, about language and communication, and about the way in which languages are learned.

Therefore, our purpose in writing this book is to share with you, in nontechnical terms, the kinds of insights that will enable you to become a better foreign language learner. We examine such questions as

- What is the nature of language and communication?
- How to define objectives for language study?
- How to plan one's language study?
- How best to manage the language-learning process?

With your help, we will also examine *you!* That is, we will ask you to consider what *you* bring to the language learning process: *your* specific knowledge and abilities, *your* personal goals, and *your* motivation. In short, what we do is provide you with the means to become the kind of foreign language learner *you* want to be.

We would like to thank the following people who gave us helpful comments for the Second Edition:

Anna Uhl Chamot, *Georgetown University*
Con Hamel, *College of Saint Benedict*
Montserrat Vilarrubla, *Illinois State University*

ℱOREWORDS

Comments on the First Edition

I was pleased to have the chance to go through the manuscript of *How to Be a More Successful Language Learner.*

Unfortunately, in the United States today we are not learning foreign languages as we should, and there has developed even a fear of learning foreign languages. There is a surprising attitude that Americans are somehow less able to learn foreign languages than people in other countries. This is, of course, a myth, but a widely held myth. And it is a myth that this book helps to destroy. Any student who follows the advice of this book will be a better language student.

I applaud this endeavor, and my only regret is that I didn't have an opportunity to read a book like this before I became a language student during my college days.

> *The Honorable Paul Simon*
> *Senate*
> *Congress of the United States*

I am happy to write an endorsement of Joan Rubin's and Irene Thompson's *How to Be a More Successful Language Learner,* which clearly meets a need we in the profession have felt for a long time and have attempted to answer in various ways. This new book can take its place alongside Moulton's *Linguistic Guide to Language Learning* and is, moreover, shorter, handier, and more explicitly aimed at the student than was its predecessor.

In my view, foreign language professionals have no worthier mission in life than to teach our students that all languages (and all cultures) are equal and are equally valid ways of organizing experience. A basic point, yet subtle enough to require explicit attention. The point is masterfully made by Rubin and Thompson. Their organization is clear, the examples well chosen, the material neither too heavy nor too light.

Not surprisingly, some teachers are still poorly informed and uncertain about linguistics. They will benefit from reading this book on their own. They will then, I predict, be eager to share its insightful perceptions with their students.

> *Richard I. Brod*
> *Director, Foreign Language Programs*
> *Modern Language Association of America*

Reading the manuscript of *How to Be a More Successful Language Learner* by Joan Rubin and Irene Thompson has been a most exciting experience for me. Although the book addresses the language learner, there is no question that it is a valuable resource for the teacher as well. The book deals with many complex issues of language learning with sparkling clarity. The most recent discoveries in language acquisition research are explained in a manner easily understood by even the most uninitiated layperson. Psycholinguistics, sociolinguistics, the Sapir-Whorf hypothesis, nondefensive learning, learner-centered learning, multidisciplinary approaches, the socio-affective filter, acculturation, the psychodynamic monitor, creative construction, humanistic classrooms, individual learning styles, learner needs, pragmatics, caretaker language, formulaic expressions: all these form the basis of the book. In addition, the proficiency ratings of the Department of State's Foreign Service Institute and the American Council on the Teaching of Foreign Languages are very clearly described. Whereas many books confuse the reader, this book communicates.

In short, *How to Be a More Successful Language Learner* is a superb book, suitable for learner and teacher alike. It is a book that should be distributed as widely as possible, as rapidly as possible. It lends impetus to our realization of the increasing need for foreign language competence in an interdependent world. It will contribute to the solution of our pressing problems in the teaching and learning of foreign languages, as well as in the teaching of English to speakers of other languages. Domestically, it will contribute to the furthering of equal educational opportunities for people of all ages and walks of life. Internationally, it will contribute to cross-cultural understanding in the interest of world peace. I strongly recommend the book to faculty and students alike.

Professor James E. Alatis
Dean, School of Languages and Linguistics
Georgetown University
Executive Director Emeritus
Teachers of English to Speakers of Other Languages (TESOL)

PART ONE

BEFORE YOU BEGIN

CHAPTER 1

You, the Language Learner

EVERYTHING DEPENDS ON YOU

You, the language learner, are the most important factor in the language learning process. Success or failure will, in the end, be determined by what you yourself contribute. Many learners tend to blame teachers, circumstances, and teaching materials for their lack of success, when the most important reason for their lack of success can ultimately be found in themselves. There are several learner traits that are relevant to learning a foreign language, and they usually appear in combination. A positive combination of these traits is probably more important than any single trait by itself.

It is important to realize that there is no stereotype of "the good language learner." There are, instead, many individual traits that contribute to success, and there are also many individual ways of learning a foreign language. People can compensate for the absence of one trait by relying more heavily on another and by accentuating their strengths to compensate for their weaknesses. There is no conclusive evidence that any one of the traits described below is more important than another, particularly over long periods of language study. The descriptions in this chapter are intended to help you analyze your predispositions. As a result, you may better understand how to enhance your learning by emphasizing your strengths and minimizing the effects of your weaknesses.

AGE AND FOREIGN LANGUAGE LEARNING

Age Has Its Advantages

Some people think that the best time to begin studying a foreign language is in childhood and that the younger you are, the easier it is to learn another language. While it is true that an early start allows people to pursue language study over longer periods of time, there is little evidence that children in language classrooms learn foreign languages any better than adults (people over age 15) in similar classroom situations. In fact, adults have many advantages over children: better memories, more efficient ways of organizing information, longer attention spans, better study habits, and greater ability to handle complex mental tasks. Adults are often better motivated than children; they see learning a foreign language as necessary for their education or career. In addition, adults are particularly sensitive to the correctness of grammar and appropriateness of vocabulary, two factors that receive great attention in most formal language classrooms.

Age Has Its Disadvantages

Adults usually want to learn a foreign language in a hurry, unlike children, who can devote many years to language mastery. Also, adults have complex communication needs that extend beyond the mere ability to carry on simple conversations. Adults need to be able to argue, persuade, express concern, object, explain, and present information about complex matters that pertain to their life, interests, work, or education. Because most adults do not like to appear foolish, they often deny themselves opportunities to practice for fear of making mistakes, of not getting their message across, or of appearing ridiculously incompetent. In addition, adults have more trouble than children in making new friends who speak the foreign language.

What About a Foreign Accent?

One example usually given to support the notion of children's superiority as language learners is their ability to pick up an authentic accent. It is usually observed that children of immigrants learn to speak the language of their adopted country without an accent, whereas their parents rarely do. It is also observed that even adults with high need and motivation, such as diplomats, rarely learn a foreign language without retaining some of their native accent. In a sense, the same is true in sports; to learn well the complex coordination of the hundreds of muscles needed to play tennis, swim, or figure skate, a person has to start young. Most champions begin training at an early age. There are examples of strong competitors who entered their sport after childhood, but they are the exception, not the rule. The same is true of adults who acquire native-like accents in a foreign language.

Taken together, the disadvantages of age are clearly offset by advantages. By properly combining positive traits and effective strategies, you *can* indeed master a foreign language—as lots of adults do.

The Best Time to Learn is Now

The best time for you to learn a foreign language is when your need is clearest and when you have sufficient time. If you are strongly motivated to study a foreign language and if you have the time to do it, the best time to begin is *now*.

LANGUAGE LEARNING APTITUDE

Foreign Language Aptitude

A person's cognitive predisposition to learn a foreign language is commonly referred to as *aptitude*. Aptitude is another way of saying "knack for languages," and like "having a good ear for languages," it is one of those myths used to explain why some people succeed while others fail. Strictly speaking, language learning aptitude is the cognitive capacity to learn a foreign language. In a classroom situation, a person with high language aptitude can usually master foreign language material faster and better than someone with lower aptitude. Thus, several studies show a strong relationship between language aptitude and grades in foreign language courses.

What Can a Language Aptitude Test Tell Us?

There are several standardized tests that measure language learning aptitude. They predict how fast and how well an individual can learn foreign languages under formal classroom conditions, when the emphasis is on *grammatical accuracy* and *memorization*. However, these tests may not be such good predictors of how well people can learn to communicate in a foreign language, especially if they have the opportunity to practice in real-life situations. In other words, language aptitude tests may predict ability to learn formally and analytically, but they may not be as reliable in measuring the ability to learn unconsciously and intuitively.

Language success may ultimately depend on persistence. You may have the potential to be a brilliant language learner, but if you fail to put effort into it, chances are you will not learn much. A good combination of talent and perseverance is ideal.

PSYCHOLOGICAL PREDISPOSITIONS

A number of psychological traits appear to be related to successful language learning. One of them, motivation, is so important that it is discussed separately in Chapter 3. In this chapter we examine several other traits that have a significant effect on language mastery.

Attitude

Emotions are important. If aptitude is an intellectual trait, then attitude is an emotional one. It may have to do with the way learners feel about the foreign culture and its people. They may admire the culture and want to learn more about it by becoming fluent in the foreign language. Or they may like the people who speak the language and wish to be accepted by them. Research has shown a definite relationship between attitudes and success when foreign language learners have an opportunity to know people who speak the language they are studying. Such positive attitudes usually help learners maintain their interest long enough to achieve their goals. Thus, if you find France and the French people attractive, and if you wish to learn more about them or wish to become more like them, you are likely to succeed at learning French.

However, some people are remarkably successful in mastering a language without feeling especially drawn to the country or the people who speak it. They may need the language for academic or career purposes, so their attitude is purely pragmatic. These two attitudes are not mutually exclusive; it is entirely possible that a person may want to learn Spanish because he or she wants to understand the Spanish people better *and* wants to study or work in Spain. More important than specific attitude is that the language learner experience a real need to communicate in the foreign language.

Personality

Extroversion. It should not be surprising that personality influences the way a person goes about learning a foreign language. Although we cannot, at present, sketch the ideal language learning personality, several traits appear to be related to success. Of these, extroversion is repeatedly mentioned as a positive trait. When everything else is equal, sociable people who use every opportunity to talk with native speakers may be more successful, because by initiating and maintaining contacts they have more chances to hear and use the new language.

Inhibition. People who are painfully aware of their limitations and worry about their ability to use the language are usually less willing to engage in either classroom practice or in real-world communication. Shyness and inhibition can stand in the way of progress in speaking (per-

haps less in the way of reading) a foreign language. They can also pre-
vent a person from taking risks or seizing opportunities to practice and
learn. Fear of making a mistake or being misunderstood can keep a learner from adopting an open-minded, active, and creative approach to language learning. Everything else being equal, persons who have an open,
receptive attitude towards the foreign language, who are not afraid to use
it, and who feel at ease in foreign language situations are more likely to
learn from their language experiences.

Tolerance of ambiguity. Tolerance of ambiguity allows a person
to reconcile and accommodate ideas that may be contradictory or information that may be inconsistent. A person who is tolerant of ambiguity
does not see everything in terms of black and white and does not put
information in airtight compartments. Such a person is willing to accept
the fact that there are many shades of gray and that uncertainty and
inconsistency must be accommodated. Tolerance of ambiguity has been
noted as an asset in learning a foreign language because there are so many
inconsistencies in language rules that even native speakers cannot always
agree on correct usage and linguists cannot explain certain language phe-
nomena. Also, whether a turn of speech is right or wrong may depend
on the situation rather than on an ironclad rule. Persons who can accept
an evasive answer such as "Well, I suppose you could say it that way under
certain circumstances" are more likely to have an open, flexible system for
accommodating new information as their knowledge of the language
increases.

Learning Style

Rules or risks? Learning a foreign language is just one form of
learning in general; therefore, each individual will employ the approach
that he or she usually applies to other learning situations. When it comes
to foreign languages, one kind of learner prefers a highly structured
approach with much explanation in the mother tongue, graded exercises, constant correction, and careful formulation of rules. This type of
learner is very analytical, reflective, and reluctant to say anything in the
foreign language that is not grammatically perfect. This person is a rule
learner. A second type of learner relies more on intuition, the gathering of
examples, and imitation. He or she is willing to take risks. There is no
evidence that one type of learner is more successful than the other. What
is more important is that the learner's style be appropriate to the particular task. If the task is to communicate orally in a real-life situation, then
risk taking is in order. If the task is to say or write something correctly,
then rules should be consulted.

It is helpful for each learner's preferences to be accommodated in the
classroom. You may thus wish to examine your own preferences and communicate them to your teacher. For instance, if you feel that you need

rules, you may be quite uncomfortable in a classroom dedicated to imitation and repetition of dialogues, and should ask the teacher for more explanations. If, on the other hand, you feel that you learn more from being exposed to the language and from making your own inferences, you may feel ill at ease in a classroom where the teacher painstakingly explains the new grammar in your native language, and you should ask the teacher for more practice in speaking.

Eye or ear? When learning a foreign language, some students depend more on their eyes; others depend on their ears. Some learners feel that they learn better if they can see the language written out, but others prefer to listen to tapes and records. It is not clear to what extent "eye-mindedness" and "ear-mindedness" are related to foreign language mastery. You may want to experiment to find out whether a single method or a combination of the two works best for you.

PAST EXPERIENCES

Is There a Foreign Language in Your Past?

Previous experiences with foreign language study may influence future attempts. If, on the one hand, a person has had a favorable experience studying one language and believes that he or she learned something valuable, that person will be predisposed to study another language and will expect to succeed. On the other hand, if an individual's first experiences with a foreign language were not particularly pleasant or successful, he or she will tend to expect the next language learning experience to be just as stressful and unfruitful as the first. Such a person should examine the reasons for the earlier lack of success. Perhaps it was due to a teacher whom the learner did not like, a textbook that was not particularly helpful, or a method that clashed with the learner's learning preferences. Or perhaps it was due to the learner's own inexperience, absence of motivation, or lack of good reasons for studying the particular language. Chances are that these conditions will not be repeated or can be avoided the second time around. The best strategy, then, is simply to wipe the slate clean and approach the study of the next language as a completely new experience.

In addition, keep in mind that people get better at whatever they do over a long period of time. In other words, based on past experience, *they learn how to learn.* People who have learned several languages usually report that each became successively easier to master, particularly if the languages were related. So don't be surprised when the star performer in your class tells you that it is his or her third or even fourth language.

CHAPTER 2

The Language Learning Process

As you begin the exciting and challenging task of learning a new language, you should have an understanding of the process and how it may affect you.

Language Learning is a Long Process

No matter what your goals, language learning takes a long time, much longer than you may have ever anticipated. This is true in part because languages are complex systems of sounds, words, grammar, and ways of expressing meaning. Each system is different and requires reorganization of your thinking, lots of exposure, and a tremendous amount of practice. It takes time for your mind to make the appropriate connections and to retain them so that you can retrieve them quickly when needed. In order to make the process effective, you will need to learn the language *in small bits but in a consistent manner.* It is more effective if you spend thirty minutes or so on your study every day than if you try to cram a lot of studying into one long session. You need to be very regular in your study habits so that the process of internalizing the new system can take effect.

Language Learning is a Process of Successive Approximation

When you learn a new language, you create a new system in your head and adopt a new set of rules for communicating and behaving. Every time you work on the new language you need to revise your understanding of its system, taking new information and new observations into account. You create the new system by establishing rules based on what you already know and then noting whether these rules work when you try to use them.

An example comes from our understanding of the way some children learn their first language. For instance, when children first learn English, they may hypothesize that there is a pattern for the present and the past tenses, such as **walk-walked, help-helped, ask-asked**. Based on this pattern, young children produce the form **goed**. But after parental correction and/or observation, children come to recognize that the correct form is *went*. It is important to note that in this process of building the verb system, children form hypotheses, test them, and later amend these hypotheses. This process is called *successive approximation*.

Because language learning consists of constructing a system through hypothesis formation and revision, errors are a natural part of the learning process. The important point is that learners need to form these hypotheses but also to be on the lookout to revise them.

Language Learning May Affect You Emotionally

Many adults feel quite uncomfortable when they begin studying a new language. Many say that they feel like children or that they feel stupid because there are so few things that they can say. Others feel so frustrated that they may want to give up. These feelings occur because adults have a real need to communicate complicated thoughts in an effective manner and because they are impatient with the length of time it takes to learn how to do this in another language. People often note that children seem to learn languages easily. This is true in large part because children do not have very complicated thoughts to express and because they usually communicate about the *here and now*.

Learning a New Language May Be Especially Difficult for Some People

Research indicates that there is a small number of individuals who experience great difficulties in learning foreign languages because they may have some subtle processing difficulties in their native language, difficulties that they have learned to overcome and compensate for. If you suspect that you are one of these individuals, ask yourself the following questions: (1) Did you experience difficulties with learning to read, write, and spell your *first* language? (2) Did you receive special help with these difficulties? (3) Were you ever enrolled in a foreign language class in which you tried *very hard* and in which most students did *much better* than you did? If this sounds like you, you will probably learn better in highly structured classes that focus directly and explicitly on the structure of the foreign language, that practice the language through simultaneous reading, writing, listening, and speaking, and that present new material in small increments with frequent review. If you fit this profile, you will probably take much longer to reach your goals than do other learners.

As an adult, you will need to remember that learning a language effectively is a long process and one that includes hypothesis formation, hypothesis revision, and many errors along the way. Let this realization help you come to terms with your feelings and help you treat yourself more kindly!

CHAPTER 3

Clarifying Your Objectives

WHY STUDY A FOREIGN LANGUAGE?

There are many reasons for learning a foreign language, and there is no doubt that having a good reason firmly in mind will enhance your chances for success. Most people need strong motivation to attack the complex task of mastering a foreign language. In general, people tend to study foreign languages for a combination of reasons that usually complement each other; a person may *need* to learn a foreign language in connection with work or study, but that person may also *enjoy* studying foreign languages for their own sake.

- *Professional.* Sometimes, a person needs to learn a foreign language in connection with a job. Communicating in a foreign language is an integral part of the work of international business people, foreign service officers, interpreters, foreign language teachers, and many other professionals.
- *Educational.* Frequently, a person needs to learn a foreign language in order to satisfy an educational requirement imposed by a school, college, or university; to use materials and resources available in another language; or to study in a foreign country.
- *Social.* Many people want to learn a foreign language in order to communicate on a primarily social level with speakers of other languages, to get to know them, and to establish relationships with them. We all live in an increasingly diverse world in which our next-door neighbors, colleagues, and fellow students may be speak-

ers of other languages. In addition, more and more people today travel outside their own countries and need to have linguistic skills in order to get their needs met.

- *Personal.* People often want to learn a foreign language for personal enrichment, to satisfy their curiosity about a country and its culture, to find a fulfilling hobby, or to seek their roots.

The more reasons you have for studying a foreign language, the more motivated you will be! Motivation, in turn, will translate into willingness to pursue your language study over a longer period of time.

WHAT ARE YOUR OBJECTIVES?

Decide What You Need to Be Able to Do

Your chances for successfully learning a foreign language are further enhanced if you take charge of the situation: that is, if *you* determine what *you* want to learn. This approach will help you select a foreign language program, or to adjust the program you are already in. Having objectives firmly in mind will also help you select suitable materials and activities. For instance, while your teacher's objective may be to teach a certain number of grammatical constructions and vocabulary items found in your textbook, your personal goal may be to learn to communicate with native speakers about simple, everyday matters. Unless the classroom goals are filtered through your personal ones, they will remain simply lessons in the book, hours spent in class, and class preparation that may not relate to your personal goals at all, or relate to them in a very indirect way. The extent to which you pursue your own objectives and adapt the objectives of the language course to your own may determine your ultimate success. Thus, you should translate the classroom objective "Learn the dialog *At the store*" into your own functional objective, "I should be able to make purchases at the store."

Such self-determination can also be exercised in the case of pronunciation, grammar, and vocabulary. You can decide, for instance, whether it is important for you to have good pronunciation in a foreign language, and allocate your efforts accordingly. For example, if you are going to use the foreign language mostly for reading, it is not important for you to have a good accent, but you will need to concentrate on vocabulary building. On the other hand, if you are planning to do a lot of speaking, you will need to concentrate on both pronunciation and grammar.

However, keep in mind that your objectives may change as your level of mastery grows, because previously difficult objectives may seem more attainable and because changes in your work, life-style, or attitude may occur.

Keep Objectives Realistic

As in all complex and long-term enterprises, your chances for success in language learning are vastly improved if you set realistic goals that can be attained over time. People often approach the study of a foreign language with nothing more than a vague "I want to learn Russian (German, Japanese)" to guide them. Since they do not have a clear idea of how complex language learning is, they often expect to be able to understand, speak, read, and write a foreign language after a relatively short period of study. When they find themselves unable to communicate with native speakers about themselves, their work, studies, interests, or current events, unable to write a friendly note or business letter, unable to read a newspaper article or to follow a TV or radio program, they often become disillusioned and blame themselves, the teachers, the program, or the textbook for their lack of success. They may discontinue their study of the foreign language altogether and acquire a negative attitude toward foreign language study in general.

Such negative outcomes can be avoided if learners realize that language learning entails a series of stages of achievement from the simple to the more complex, and that success at each stage requires a certain amount of practice in the skills you want to acquire. Learners should thus structure their approach and measure their success accordingly. By setting modest, realistic objectives for yourself along the way, you can more easily sustain your motivation and interest.

When setting objectives, it is important to be realistic about the degree of your commitment and the amount of time you are able or willing to devote to language study. For instance, if you are an English speaker and intend to spend two years in college studying a foreign language, it is realistic to expect to attain a very minimal level of speaking proficiency (e.g., ability to "survive" in tourist-type situations involving talking to native speakers who are accustomed to dealing with tourists). It is also realistic to expect to be able to read very simple prose in a language closely related to English, such as Spanish, French, or Italian. It is unrealistic to expect to be able to discuss current events and abstract topics or to read sophisticated prose.

Some Languages May Take Longer to Learn

In setting goals, it is important to keep in mind that some languages take more time to learn than others, depending on their degree of relatedness to your native language, complexity of grammar, and type of writing system. For instance, the U.S. government experience indicates that whereas it might take a speaker of English approximately six months of full-time language study to achieve professional proficiency in speaking French, Spanish, Italian, or Portuguese, it will take a year in Russian, Czech, or Polish, and two years in Arabic, Japanese, or Korean. Thus, if you are planning to study a "difficult" language,you should budget your time accordingly.

Different Objectives for Different Skills

Learners often expect to be able to speak, understand, read, and write a foreign language even though they have had experience in the language with only one or two of these skills. It is important to realize that although there is a good deal of carry-over from one skill to another, each skill needs separate attention and practice in order to develop. For instance, if your study of a foreign language stresses reading and grammar practice, it is doubtful that you will be readily able to understand native speech or to speak the language yourself. Conversely, if your language experience stresses speaking and listening comprehension, you may not be able to read newspapers or write personal or business letters. The point is that one must decide whether one needs all the skills, some combination of them, or just one.

One of the main reasons for setting a goal is that it will help you to choose activities that are important to you and prompt you to spend less time and effort on those that do not help you achieve your purposes.

SPEAKING OBJECTIVES

How Well Do You Want to Speak?

Suppose that your reason for studying a foreign language is to learn to speak it. Since learning to speak is a complex skill, you should set step-by-step objectives for yourself. As mentioned previously, these objectives should be reasonable for the language you have chosen ("easy" vs. "difficult") and for the amount of time you have available.

In order to think of speaking ability in terms of stages, it might be useful to adopt the system used by the American Council on the Teaching of Foreign Languages (ACTFL) and the U.S. government. The system is designed to evaluate people's speaking ability, regardless of how, where, or for how long they have studied a foreign language. The definition of each proficiency level is applicable to any language, although, as mentioned earlier, the amount of time to reach a given level varies widely from language to language. These ratings are called S-ratings (S stands for speaking). They range from Novice (= Government S-0), no functional speaking ability at all, to Educated Native Speaker (= Government S-5). For our purposes, the more central ratings, namely 1, 2, 3, and 4, are more useful.

Experience shows that it takes progressively more time and effort to move from one level to the next as one moves up the hierarchy. The hierarchy of levels has been described as an inverted pyramid or, if you prefer, an ice cream cone. As you can see from Figure 1, it takes less language to fill the layers at the bottom of the inverted pyramid than those on top.

FIGURE 1 The Inverted Pyramid of Language Proficiency

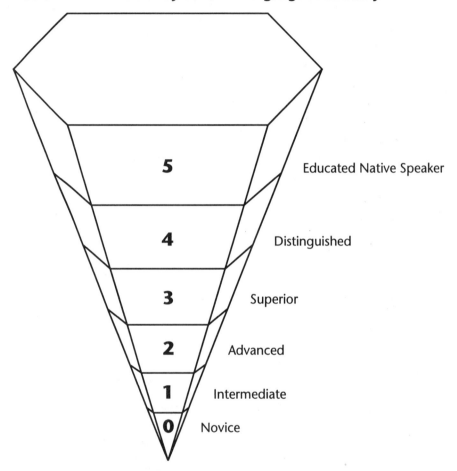

Novice (S 0): Prefunctional Level. This is the first entry level into the language. You will have to go through this stage in order to later start gaining *functional* speaking ability. This stage is characterized by the ability to communicate minimally in highly predictable common daily settings with *learned* material, primarily formulaic phrases such as greetings and expressions of thanks. Novice speakers can produce discrete words or phrases which they rarely combine into sentences. They may be difficult to understand, even for those native speakers who are accustomed to nonnative speakers attempting to speak their language. In short, Novice speakers would have a hard time surviving in the country where the language is spoken.

Government people parachute into Superior situations and miss stage 1 + 2

Intermediate (S 1): Survival Level. This is the first *functional* level that can serve you if you want to survive on your own in the country where the foreign language is spoken. For instance, you may need to be able to get a room in a hotel, tell a taxi driver where you want to go, order a meal in a restaurant, handle a simple shopping situation, ask for directions, and give basic information about yourself, such as your name, age, address, and occupation. You should be able to handle the basic courtesies, such as addressing people appropriately, and thanking them, when necessary. Normally, people at this level have limited grammar and vocabulary, speak hesitantly in short or incomplete sentences, and make all sorts of mistakes in pronunciation, vocabulary, and grammar. They are usually incapable of a sustained conversation and are best understood by native listeners who are accustomed to dealing with foreigners, such as teachers, tourist guides, and airline clerks.

If this level will satisfy your needs, then learning the vocabulary and grammar associated with "survival" topics as well as prefabricated sentences and ways to get your conversation partner to help you is the way to go. Complex grammatical constructions and abstract vocabulary can wait.

Advanced (S 2): Limited Working Proficiency. This is the first true *utility* level in speaking because it will allow you to work, study, and socialize using the foreign language, albeit still in a limited way. At this level you will be able, without going into details, to describe your job and the organization you work for, handle simple job-related inquiries, direct people to the right office, answer the telephone, and handle other situations that involve complications in the foreign language. You can begin to develop friendly relationships with native speakers since you will be able to sustain conversations about a variety of personal and factual topics and since you will be understood by native listeners without difficulty.

To achieve this level, you need more grammar, more vocabulary, and greater fluency than for achieving mere "survival" ability. You will still make a number of mistakes and grope for words and expressions, but you will usually be able to sustain conversations.

If this is your goal, you should make sure that your language training includes some specific work-related learning materials and simulations of situations in which you may actually have to use the foreign language. You should also try to talk to native speakers in order to learn how to manage conversations. Experience shows that this is usually the highest level of proficiency attained by persons who have studied the language formally without having had an opportunity to live in the country or in a community where it is spoken.

Superior (S 3): Professional Proficiency. If you have a very strong interest in the language and the country in which it is spoken and if you need the language to carry out fully the responsibilities of your job, you may aspire to greater mastery of the spoken language than so far described. You may wish to be able to participate in conversations with native speakers on a variety of topics, including professional ones, with relative fluency and ease. At this point, you will need to have mastered all the grammatical features of the language and enough vocabulary to cover a wide variety of topics. Chances are that you will still make occasional mistakes and search for the right word or expression, but this should not affect your fluency too much since you will be able to circumlocute and paraphrase with ease.

Should the attainment of such a level of proficiency be your goal, you will have to study the language for an extended period of time. Experience shows that this level is rarely attainable without an extended stay in the country where the language is spoken. Therefore, you should plan on a relatively prolonged period of residence abroad.

If you reach this level of mastery, you can become a full participant in any communicative situation involving the foreign language. You have arrived, so to speak. Congratulations!

Distinguished Proficiency (S 4): Near Native Proficiency. If your aspirations are really high and you wish to be able to speak the foreign language almost like a native speaker, with a great degree of fluency, grammatical accuracy, precision of vocabulary, and idiomaticity, you will need many years of study and an extended stay in the country where the language is spoken. As a rule, very few learners can attain such a high level. But it is a worthy goal if one is ambitious and patient enough.

You can see that people move from one level to the next as they continue their study of a foreign language in a combination of formal and informal settings. If you can identify the level you want or need to achieve, you will be better able to focus your efforts. You will also feel more positive about your achievements because you will be able to appreciate them more.

READING OBJECTIVES

Like speaking, reading can be thought of in terms of levels of difficulty. Depending upon your desires and needs, you may aim for one of the following levels of reading proficiency, called the R-levels (R stands for "reading").

Novice (R 0): Prefunctional Level. Suppose that you want to take a short trip to a foreign country and would like to be able to read a few words that are strongly supported by context, such as street signs, menus, and forms. If you are studying a language related to your own and one that uses the same writing system, you will be able to do this in a relatively short period of time.

Intermediate (R 1): Survival Level. This level describes you, if you want to be able to read, with heavy reliance on a dictionary, simple texts such as newspaper announcements about *who, when, where, why,* that contain the most common words and the simplest grammatical constructions. If you are a speaker of a Western European language and are studying a language related to your own, this level can be achieved in a relatively short time and usually forges ahead of speaking ability. In languages with different scripts, such as Chinese or Japanese, the situation may be reversed, and it can take longer to learn to read than to speak.

Advanced (R 2): Limited Working Proficiency. If your job requires some reading ability in a foreign language, you will probably need to be able to understand the main ideas and some details in uncomplicated but authentic prose that deals with straightforward topics and contains many common words and familiar sentence patterns, such as news reports, encyclopedia entries, and short biographies, etc. People at this level usually can also read simple short stories with a clear story line. At this level, you will have to do a good deal of rereading and will occasionally misread. Your reading comprehension will be heavily dependent on subject matter knowledge.

Superior (R 3): Professional Proficiency. This is the level you need if you want to be able to read with almost complete comprehension and at normal speed most texts intended for educated native readers of the language you are studying, for example, literary texts and expository prose on a wide variety of topics and of different genres (editorials, correspondence, general reports, technical material in your professional field, official documents, and political commentary). You will have to know a good deal about the target language culture in order to achieve this level of comprehension.

Distinguished (R 4): Near Native Proficiency. If you want to be able to read as quickly and effortlessly in a foreign language as you can read in your native language, this is the level for you because you will be able to read anything published in the foreign language without using a dictionary. You will be able to read all styles and forms of the language pertinent to professional and academic needs, including intellectually challenging and artistic prose. You will be able to understand nuances and subtleties, cultural and literary references and associations, and have an appreciation of humor, irony, and sarcasm.

LISTENING OBJECTIVES

Like speaking and reading, listening comprehension can also be thought of in terms of levels of achievement, ranging from an ability to understand a few words from speech directly aimed at you to the ability to completely understand lectures, radio/TV, movies, public speeches, and plays.

Novice (L 0): Prefunctional. This is the entry level into the foreign language at which learners begin to identify individual words and phrases that they have studied in face-to-face speaking situations. Much repetition is often required.

Intermediate (L 1): Survival Level. This is the absolute minimum level of comprehension you will need if you want to survive on your own in a restricted number of situations that deal with the immediate surroundings and that are strongly supported by context such as is sufficient for getting around, making purchases, or ordering meals. At this level, you may also begin to understand bits and pieces of radio/TV announcements and news reports dealing with familiar topics and containing familiar vocabulary.

Advanced (L 2): Limited Working Proficiency. You need this level as a minimum if you have to work or study in a foreign country. At this level, you should be able to understand most face-to-face conversations in which you are a participant, as well as simple TV and radio newscasts and short lectures on well-known events and topics. You will still be missing quite a few details.

Superior (L 3): Professional Proficiency. If you want to understand academic lectures, speeches, movies, and all types of media coverage, this is the level you will have to attain. You will need to spend some time in the foreign country before your understanding reaches this level.

Distinguished (L 4): Near Native Proficiency. If you want to be able to understand the foreign language almost as well as you can understand your own, this is the level for you. At this level, people understand all forms and styles of speech, including plays, academic and professional debates, literary readings, business negotiations, puns, and jokes. You will need to spend a good deal of time in the foreign country before you can reach this level of understanding.

WRITING OBJECTIVES

In some ways, objectives for writing resemble those for speaking since both require productive use of language. However, people do a lot less writing than they do speaking, so writing objectives can be more limited. In some cases, people simply may not need to do any writing in the foreign language at all.

Novice (W 0): Prefunctional. This is the level at which you are merely practicing the basics of the writing system—i.e., learning to write isolated words and a few simple sentences. This type of writing is usually done in beginning language courses, mostly as a support activity for learning grammar and vocabulary. In the real world, this is the level you need in order to fill out simple travel documents and hotel registration forms.

Depending on the writing system, this level can take a relatively short or quite a long time to achieve.

Intermediate (W 1): Survival Level. This is the level you need if you want to be able to write short messages, and postcards, and take down basic information from simple telephone conversations by using simple grammatical structures and vocabulary. Many mistakes in grammar, vocabulary, spelling, and punctuation can be expected.

Advanced (W 2): Limited Working Proficiency. This is a level at which your writing could be used in working or studying in a foreign country. You should be able to handle routine social and some limited business correspondence, and take lecture notes.

Superior (W 3): Professional Proficiency. This is the level you need if you have to be able to write for professional purposes, such as all kinds of business correspondence, reports, and proposals. You will still need a native speaker to check your writing.

Distinguished Proficiency (W 4): Near Native Proficiency. This is the level for people who want to be able to write intellectually and linguistically complex prose, such as letters to the editor, articles for professional journals, and essays.

CHAPTER 4

Planning Your Language Study

Once you have decided what your objectives are, you will need to find the optimal learning environment in which they can be achieved. There are two basic environments in which a language can be learned: informal and formal. When a language is learned primarily through immersion into the foreign speech community, we refer to it as an *informal* setting. When a language is learned mainly with a teacher and a textbook (e.g., in a classroom), we call it a *formal* setting.

INFORMAL SETTINGS

The Language Community

Learning a foreign language in a community where it is spoken has its advantages and disadvantages, because outside the classroom, communication is generally not organized around the learner's needs. The language to which the learner is exposed is not organized around grammatical topics, and the vocabulary is not presented in an organized fashion. However, an informal environment does offer a great deal of information about the nature of interaction and about appropriate ways of speaking. It usually also offers clues to the meaning of a conversation, since the setting, the relationship between participants, and the topic are generally clear. Further, and more importantly, it offers one of the strongest reasons for learning—the need to communicate. Most people study a language in order to talk to other people. In informal environments in which only the foreign language is spoken, the need to make oneself understood is crucial. Hence, informal environments offer unlimited opportunities for practice as well as instant reward—being understood. Punishment is just as instant and obvious: one fails to communicate the intended message.

Informal Language Learning

In informal settings, learners are neither particularly aware that they are learning, nor are they generally able to describe what they have learned. Since the primary use of language in informal settings is communication, people learning another language in such settings usually go through a number of stages before attaining mastery. Learners in informal settings often go through a silent period; they just listen to the new language and do not speak until they feel ready. In the early stages, they make lots of mistakes and rely heavily on their first language, on gestures, and on the help of their conversational partners. With additional practice, most of them begin to make fewer mistakes, and rely less on their native tongue and on their partners. A certain percentage of people continue to learn more and more words and make gains in fluency, but continue to make grammar mistakes. We sometimes refer to this kind of language as "fossilized." This is not uncommon among immigrants who come to a new country as adults. Eventually, however, most informal learners reach a stage at which their speech approximates that of native speakers.

FORMAL SETTINGS

The Classroom

In formal environments, learning activities are generally graded, simplified, arranged around specific topics, and accompanied by presentation of specific grammatical structures and vocabulary lists. This situation provides an opportunity to learn a controlled sequence, with the teacher usually providing feedback by correcting mistakes and emphasizing the conscious learning of rules. The mother tongue is often used for explanation and communication between teacher and students about anything that is not contained in the lesson.

Formal Language Learning

Formal classroom environments do not always offer continuous strong motivation to communicate or the opportunity to observe the way language is used in real life. The emphasis is often on *knowing* about the language, on being able to produce correct sentences on cue, and on knowing why they are correct or incorrect. When students speak in the classroom, teachers often want them to produce correct grammar, with the content of the message often considered secondary and occasionally totally irrelevant. After all, when one is practicing the plural forms of nouns, it is relatively unimportant whether one uses vegetables or pieces of furniture as long as one does so correctly. The focus is not on *what* is expressed, but on *how* it is expressed. In real-world settings, however, confusing noun endings is much less serious than confusing vegetables with furniture.

In formal settings, people often learn a particular structure and then practice it in different contexts. Once the "structure of the day" is mastered, the teacher proceeds to the next, until the students have completed a list of structures considered essential. However, there is no guarantee that the learners will be able to use these structures when they need to convey a message and are concentrating on its meaning. In fact, we know that most learners who study a foreign language only in a classroom have difficulty communicating in the foreign language although they may know a great deal about it.

However, formal settings do have certain advantages. With their emphasis on accuracy, they allow learners to become aware of the rules of the language. This, in turn, helps them to develop an internal alarm system (a "monitor") that will allow them to notice their own mistakes and to self-correct.

COMBINING FORMAL AND INFORMAL SETTINGS

The Best of Two Worlds

People ask about which is more beneficial for adult learners: studying a foreign language in the classroom or using it in real-life situations. The answer to this question is, of course, that both are needed.

When beginning foreign language learners study in the classroom without a chance for real-life interaction with native speakers, their only sources of input are the teacher, the textbook, and media materials such as tapes or videos. The students benefit from error correction, explanation of rules, and graded practice, which reduce information overload and provide a certain amount of security. The instructor often makes a conscious attempt to use simplified and familiar language, and this makes the students feel successful. As the knowledge of the language increases, however, such study becomes less valuable than the use of the language outside the classroom.

If you are a beginning language learner and if you need outside motivation in order to keep studying, look for a standard classroom language course. If, however, you enjoy learning languages in their natural setting, go the informal route. Keep in mind that the usefulness of the standard language classroom decreases as you progress in the language. A high-intermediate or advanced student usually profits more from a stay in the country where the language is spoken than from continuing classroom study, especially as far as speaking and listening are concerned.

Using both settings may also be helpful. Since most adults are more comfortable in structured situations yet also need the motivation to communicate that comes from informal settings, they should try to take advantage of both environments.

INDEPENDENT STUDY

What If Nobody Teaches Your Language?

Another alternative available to language learners is independent study. In fact, it may be the only solution when the language you want to study is not taught anywhere in your geographic area, the language course you want to take is offered at an inconvenient time, or the pace of a particular language course is inappropriate for you. Should that be the case, find out if self-study materials are available for the language you are planning to study.

Are You Disciplined Enough?

Keep in mind that independent study requires a great deal of self-discipline and self-motivation. Ask yourself if you can sustain motivation on your own and, if so, for how long. If you have been successful in self-study before, you will probably be able to handle such an approach. If you have never tried independent study in the past, you might consider starting the foreign language in a regular classroom or at least finding a native speaker to work with on a regular basis.

SELECTING THE RIGHT LANGUAGE COURSE

One of the most important steps towards success in foreign language learning is selecting the course of study that's right for you. Here are some things to consider in making your decision.

Will the Course Help You Attain Your Objectives?

If you know your objectives for studying another language, be sure that the course you choose will help you attain them. Treat the selection of a language course like you treat any major purchase—read the course description, if available, consult people who have taken it, if feasible, and observe a class, if permissible. During your visit, consider the following:

- *If you want to learn how to* speak *the foreign language, does it seem likely that this course will help you achieve your objectives?* For instance, does the teacher use the foreign language to communicate with the students? Are there meaningful communicative activities, such as role plays or discussions? Are the students encouraged to use the foreign language to express their thoughts? Observe the amount of student participation. A course in which students actively participate is usually more likely to impart speaking skills than one in which the teacher does all the talking.

- *Examine the textbook.* If you want to learn to read and the textbook emphasizes dialogues and oral activities and does not contain reading passages accompanied by meaningful reading exercises, you might be better off seeking another course, if available, or you will need to acquire supplemental reading materials if there is no other course.

- *Consider the classroom pace.* Is it too slow or too fast for you? If you need to learn to speak at the S1 level in one year, it is unlikely that a class of twenty students meeting three times a week for fifty-minute sessions will get you there. Look for an intensive course that will give you many hours of practice in a short period of time.

- *See how you like the teacher and his or her approach.* You will learn to speak better from a teacher who listens patiently for the students to finish speaking, does not correct each mistake, does not finish sentences for the students, and does not interrupt with explanations.

Consider Your Learning Style

If you need outside motivation to keep studying, look for a standard classroom language course. If, however, you enjoy working steadily on your own and do not need the motivation provided by a teacher and regularly scheduled class meetings, consider a self-study or individualized course. Such programs allow you to set your own pace and require only periodic consultations with the instructor (sometimes over the telephone) and periodic visits for testing rather than regular attendance. While independent study permits you to decide how much, when, and how you will learn, it also requires you to accept full responsibility for your learning. If you are prepared to take on such responsibility, a self-instructional course might be a good idea, particularly if learning to read is more important to you than learning to speak and understand oral speech.

How Comprehensive is the Language Program?

If you are interested in long term study of a foreign language, look for a program that offers courses at all levels of proficiency. This will ensure smooth progress from one level to another, since transferring from program to program has many disadvantages, including incompatibility of approaches, materials, and amount of material covered. Institutions vary widely in their curricula, and you can avoid much frustration by choosing a program that will meet your needs well into the future. Unfortunately there are all too few extended programs in the less commonly taught languages. For these, most colleges and universities offer only one or two years of study.

How Much Language Practice Does the Program Offer?

Foreign languages can be learned in a variety of settings, including the ideal combination of formal classroom instruction and informal exposure to the language in its natural setting. Therefore, it is important that you consider the amount of practice a particular program offers outside the classroom. For instance, some intensive summer programs, such as those at Middlebury College in Vermont, require that students sign a pledge not to use English either inside or outside of the classroom. The students reside in foreign language dormitories where they speak the language among themselves and with their teachers. This arrangement provides countless hours of language practice, albeit in a setting that lacks authenticity.

Are You an Experienced Language Learner?

Consider the amount of experience you have in learning other languages. If you are a very inexperienced language learner, you may lack the learning strategies necessary for a self-instructional course. If, on the other hand, you are an experienced language learner, a self-instructional or individualized program might be just right for you.

How Commonly Taught is the Language You Want to Learn?

Finding courses in the less commonly taught languages, such as Russian, Arabic, Chinese, and Japanese, may be more difficult than finding courses in the more commonly taught languages, such as Spanish, French, and German. In these cases, you may wish to consider some form of self-instruction or even a tutor. The National Association of Self-Instructional Language Programs (see Appendix B) has a large network of institutions that offer self-study programs in many uncommonly taught languages. In addition, Ohio State University has produced individualized-study materials for a variety of languages, including such uncommonly taught ones as Arabic, Czech, Polish, Ukrainian, and Hungarian. These materials require regular testing, so you will need to arrange for someone to proctor the tests. Information about materials in the less commonly taught languages can be obtained from the Center for Applied Linguistics and from Ohio State University (see Appendix B).

How About a Tutor?

In some cases, working with a tutor will prove to be the best solution, especially if the language you wish to study is not taught in your geographical area. If you are lucky, you can find a tutor who has some language teaching experience and who knows what to do. Sometimes, however, tutors are native speakers with little language teaching experience. In such cases, it is a good idea to find a set of language materials that will tell both you and the tutor what to do. Alternatively, a well-designed self-instructional course can be used in conjunction with a tutor, who can provide you with conversational practice.

Consider Study Abroad as an Option

An increasing number of Americans study foreign languages abroad. You might consider the possibility of study abroad through a university-sponsored program, an exchange program, or some other arrangement, such as living with a family in the country where the language is spoken. Studying the language abroad may be the best way to improve language skills, particularly speaking and listening, for learners at the intermediate and advanced levels.

When looking into a language course in a foreign country, consider the duration—some courses are so short that you could not greatly improve your proficiency. Thus, a five-week language study that includes a sightseeing trip to France may be great fun and a good way to learn about France and the French people, but it probably won't significantly improve your proficiency in the French language. Experience shows that, depending on the difficulty of the language, you need at least four to six months in a country in order to have an opportunity to significantly improve your skills.

How Much Time Do You Have to Devote to Language Study?

Last but not least, be realistic about the amount of time you can spend on a foreign language. Language courses are usually very demanding and require regular study, so be sure that you can devote enough time to make the course worthwhile. As a rule of thumb, each hour of class requires two hours of study, which may include work in a language laboratory with tapes, videos, and computers, or work with classmates.

LOCATING THE RIGHT LANGUAGE COURSE

Foreign languages are widely taught. You can find instruction in several foreign languages in metropolitan areas of practically any country in the world. In the United States, Canada, and Europe, some languages are taught more commonly than others. Among these languages in the United States, Canada, and Europe are English, French, Spanish, and German. If you live in North America, you might be able to find language courses in your vicinity at one of these institutions:

- county departments of education
- community colleges
- universities
- university extension programs
- university independent study programs
- university alumni programs
- high schools
- ethnic organizations, including churches and clubs
- commercial language schools, such as Berlitz
- foreign government-sponsored organizations, such as Alliance Française
- public and educational television stations

CHAPTER 5

The Communication Process

ABOUT COMMUNICATION

The Message is Paramount

For most people, the main goal of studying a foreign language is to be able to communicate. The essence of communication is sending and receiving messages effectively and negotiating meaning. If you want to learn another language quickly and efficiently, you should keep this main goal in mind, for the other goals, such as learning grammar and vocabulary, will follow naturally.

We all learn our first language quite naturally, by focusing on this need to communicate. We learn how to send and receive messages effectively in order to accomplish our social goals. All native speakers communicate without thinking about the process. However, in order to accelerate the learning of another language, we need to become more aware of the knowledge and skills we bring to the process. By identifying and recognizing what we already know, we can more effectively guide our learning and be able to take shortcuts or recognize where we have gone wrong in expressing ourselves or in interpreting others' messages.

TWO KINDS OF MESSAGES: REFERENTIAL AND SOCIAL

Some people mistakenly think that language learning entails finding how to translate word for word from the native to the new language. Those who hold this basic misunderstanding of the communication process will find language learning next to impossible! Behind this belief is the idea that sending messages is just a matter of supplying information about something the speaker knows or wants (referential messages) and that the task is to find the exact words in another language that express this knowledge or desire.

The Same Meaning Can Be Expressed in a Variety of Ways

One of the problems with the above view is the fact is that we can say the same thing in many different ways. For example, if we wanted a window closed, we could give a direct command: "Close the window!" Or we could do so less directly by asking "Could you please close the window?" However, under other circumstances, we might choose to be quite indirect by saying "I feel cold" or "It's cold in here." The way we choose to make this request depends on the person to whom we are talking, the importance of the request, and even our mood at the time (social messages). The point is that at the same time that we share referential meanings, such as information about our knowledge or desires, we also send vital social messages. The two occur together inseparably in personal conversations. It is next to impossible to send one kind of message without the other.

There are very few situations in which referential meaning is paramount with little variation tolerated. An exceptional example of this is the exchange that takes place between an air traffic controller and a pilot. In this case, variation is not possible and basic information exchange is of the essence. On the other hand, we sometimes use language only for social purposes with little exchange of information. For example, when English speakers ask "How are you?" they don't really want to know the answer in detail. In most conversations, we send both referential and social messages at the same time, with the social side often being somewhat more important.

There is much more to language differences than mere dissimilarities in pronunciation, grammar, and vocabulary. Communication is governed by rules that specify such things as who can participate, what the social relationships are, what subjects can be discussed, who initiates the conversation, how turns are taken, who chooses the form of address, and so forth. All these vary from one speech community to another just as much as grammar and vocabulary do.

Here is an example of how word-for-word translation might mislead us and how focusing only on a referential meaning might cause us to miss the real message of a communication. In many parts of the world, it is not polite to accept an offer of more food the first time it is offered. Americans may be surprised or annoyed that their polite "no, thank you" brings yet another offer of food. When native English speakers say "no" to offers of food, they really mean "no." However, when translated into another language in another social setting, saying "no" to an offer of food may be interpreted as a polite refusal with anticipation that the real refusal will be made after the second or third offer. In fact, people in many parts of the world are reluctant to appear too greedy or childlike by accepting food or drink the first or second time it is offered. On the other hand, foreign visitors to the United States may be disappointed when their polite "no, thank you" does *not* bring a second or third offer of food. The point is that while a form may permit translation, its social meaning depends on customary use and on the associated values within a particular social context.

Finding the *appropriate* expression to use and paying attention to the *way* something is expressed are important because they are part of the messages people send and receive. Through the *form* we use, we express our feelings about a person or situation. For example, consider the distinction many languages make between the formal and familiar forms for "you" and "thou." With just a change of pronoun form, you can express contempt or respect, intimacy or distance. Further, knowing when to switch from "you" to "thou" and knowing who may initiate the switch are essential. Premature use of "thou" can nip a budding friendship or, if intentionally employed, be a serious insult. On the other hand, failure to shift from normal to familiar at the right moment can be read as standoffishness or stuffiness.

It is usually more important to find the appropriate way of expressing yourself than to be grammatically correct or to have a good pronunciation. Appropriateness in expression is linked to basic attitudes about people's social values and how people should interact with one another.

Variation is Socially Meaningful

Sending messages not only involves sharing information; it also, at the same time, involves trying to accomplish one of several social functions:

Establishing or maintaining one's social status. A British person may use phrases such as "to have one's bath" (not "to take a bath") or "ring me up" (not "give me a call") to establish that he or she is a member of the upper class. Similarly, an American who never uses colloquial expressions such as "ain't" or "gosh" or uses Latin expressions such as **"non sequitur"** or **"ad hominem"** may be working to maintain the impression that he or she is a member of an educated class.

Establishing or maintaining social group membership. A person may deliberately speak like a jazz musician to indicate membership in a jazz group, since jazz musicians have many expressions that they uniquely use. Also, in most countries it is essential for academics to speak and write in a particular way to show that they belong to the academic subculture. A third well-known example is the language of teenagers. If young people don't use the popular expressions of their generation, they are not accepted by their peers.

Showing respect or deference. In French, use of the pronoun *vous* (formal "you") indicates greater respect than use of *tu* (familiar "you"). In Chinese, people are addressed by their occupational titles to show respect, hence "Manager Wong" or "Engineer Li."

Showing intimacy. In Russian, use of diminutives indicates intimacy. Thus, friends normally use nicknames with diminutive suffixes, such as **Ninochka** (Nina) or **Boren'ka** (Boris). The greater the intimacy and affection, the greater the use of such diminutive forms. Pronouns are also used to signal intimacy. In French, use of the pronoun *tu* shows greater intimacy than use of the pronoun *vous*, and the distinction is true of Spanish, German, and all Slavic languages.

Setting yourself apart from the group. If you are normally a member of a jazz group but refuse to use its special expressions and phrases, you may be trying to show that you no longer belong to the group. When African Americans refuse to employ Black English, choosing instead the English used by middle-class whites, they may also be deliberately setting themselves apart from other African Americans.

As native speakers, we have little difficulty with referential or social meanings within our own social group because we learn early in our lives how to recognize both meanings intended by a speaker. However, once outside our own social group, we may not be as effective in sending and receiving messages, and misunderstanding may occur much more frequently as a result. This potential for misinterpreting usually increases dramatically once we speak a foreign language. As language learners, we need to be aware that misunderstanding may come from using a form inappropriately or from misinterpreting the intention of an expression. Because the form a message takes is determined so strongly by social meaning, a language learner must be sensitive to how social messages are sent in order to properly express both referential and social intentions.

THE THREE ACTIVITIES OF COMMUNICATION

There are three basic activities we engage in during the communication process: we express our intentions (send messages), we interpret intentions (receive messages), and we negotiate the intention of these messages.

Expressing Intentions

You have probably heard people say "John *says* one thing and *means* another." As a native speaker, you always need to interpret other people's messages and express your own in ways that make your communicative intent clear. This is not an easy matter, and people often ask for clarification. They frequently ask "Did I understand you to mean . . . .?" In other words, it is quite common to hear what a person says but not understand the message, either because of the way it was organized or the context in which it occurred. Sometimes, we recognize that others have misunderstood our meaning, and we may try to correct their interpretation by saying something like "What I meant to say was . . . ."

While we are learning our native language, much parental effort is directed toward teaching us how to express our intentions in a socially acceptable manner and how to interpret the intentions of others. This process begins at a very young age and, for some, continues into adulthood. An example is the often-heard parental instruction: "If you want a cookie (some milk, your doll), you will have to ask for it politely."

Because this training is such an integral part of our early language learning, we come to believe that there is certainly only one right way to send and receive messages. *Right* means that we learn to evaluate messages according to our own rules of interpretation. We may act very negatively when messages come in forms we don't understand or expect.

Learning to express our intentions in a new language involves many things. For instance, it means learning how to show agreement, when and how to hide feelings, how to make a request, how to start a friendship, how to pay a compliment, and how to accept or decline an invitation.

Interpreting Messages

Learning to interpret what others mean is also complex. Because we learn early to interpret meanings by the *form* of expression a person uses, there is much room for misunderstanding. This may lead us to make value judgments and become convinced that a speaker is insincere, dishonest, or disrespectful when we misread the intentions or the significance of a message within a social setting.

One example of the need to use and understand socially appropriate messages is in the determination of when a speaker has said **no**. In many languages and societies, people usually don't say **no** directly. Instead, they have less direct ways of expressing refusal. The nonnative speaker needs to recognize the ways in which this is done. For example, in Hispanic cultures it is considered inappropriate for servants to say **no** directly to their employers. Instead, the social norm requires the servant to reply to a request from an employer with the form **mañana**. Although a literal translation of **mañana** is "tomorrow," the most frequently intended meaning for it in this situation is simply "no." But, this is a polite **no**, since the request has not been refused directly, just postponed. A nonnative employer will wait a long time for service if he or she relies on the literal meaning of the word **mañana**.

Still another example of misinterpretation has to do with who may initiate a conversation. In some Asian languages, such as Chinese,

Japanese, or Korean, children do not usually initiate conversations with adults and do not speak unless spoken to. In contrast, American children are free, and even encouraged, to initiate conversations with adults. Similarly, whenever there is a perceived difference in status—for example, between student and teacher—the inferior usually does not initiate verbal contact. So if you are a teacher, Asian students will generally not talk to you unless you talk to them first. This, incidentally, can create the mistaken impression that Asians are passive or that they do not understand what is going on.

As foreign language learners, we need to be on the lookout for the appropriate way to express ourselves. When native speakers get angry, look confused, or laugh at our speech, it is probably because our way of expressing ourselves is inappropriate, rather than grammatically incorrect. We also need to be aware of our own possible misinterpretations of others. If we find ourselves feeling confused or angry, we need to back up and seek the source of the problem in the flow of conversation and the style of our expression. This process of interpretation and reinterpretation should not discourage us, since even in our native language we continue to improve our means of expression and techniques of understanding others throughout our lives.

Negotiating Meaning

A speaker's meaning is not always perfectly clear, and in some cases a message might be deliberately ambiguous. Hence, you will note that native speakers often negotiate meaning by asking if a particular story was meant to be a joke or if a statement was intended as a compliment or as an insult. They could also state that they don't understand a speaker's intention and need clarification. Negotiation is an important part of any communicative exchange. When speaking a foreign language, we need to discover when a statement is negotiable and how to indicate that a statement we have made is negotiable.

Negotiation is possible and, indeed, often expected in the case of invitations and in saying **no**. In American English, an invitation is sometimes issued in such a way that it cannot be negotiated—that is, the date and time are fixed. On other occasions, some seeming non-invitations can be negotiated. When someone says, "Let's get together soon," he or she is usually *not* issuing an invitation. However, the sequence could continue with the other person saying something like "I'd love to. Would you like to set up a time now?" Then the listener can negotiate the situation into an invitation.

Negotiation may also take place to determine whether a response is a definitive **no**. Recognizing when the word **no** is actually meant takes a great deal of social knowledge and learning. Children often have trouble with this, provoking their parents to express their nonnegotiable intention by saying something like, "I said **no** and that's **final**."

Expressing, interpreting, and negotiating meaning are all part of the normal communication process. As foreign language learners, we need to make sure that our messages are interpreted appropriately. We can do this by watching our listeners' facial expressions and noting whether the next comment is an appropriate reply to our intended message. Equally, we can monitor ourselves for misunderstanding by checking our own emotional responses.

Finally, we should note that monitoring a written message is much more difficult. Since we do not have the same sort of immediate feedback, we must be very careful that we express ourselves in an appropriate manner and that we have correctly interpreted the writer's intentions.

PROBLEMS IN SENDING AND RECEIVING MESSAGES

Many things get in the way of expressing and interpreting messages. In this section, we will focus on two major causes of misinterpretation: regional and social variations of expression. In the next section, we will focus on the importance of nonverbal behavior: body language, facial expressions, gestures, silence, and the like.

Note Regional Variations

First of all, it's important to bear in mind that language varies from city to city and region to region. Such differences may cause a language learner some difficulty both in understanding speakers from other areas and in being understood. Inappropriate use of regional speech can sometimes lead to humor or, worse, anger. For example, although the word **papaya** is used in most of Latin America, it is considered obscene in Cuba, where the fruit is instead called **fruta bomba**. Use of the label **papaya** in Cuba may evoke an angry reaction, although a clearly identifiable foreigner may get away with just a laugh.

Note Social Variations

Second, one needs to pay attention to variations based on social differences, since misuse of these may be amusing or insulting. Equally, hearers may miss important messages if they are unaware of the social message inherent in a turn of speech. Some examples of social variation are the following.

    Note variations according to sex, social status, social sole, or age. In Japanese, the sentence final particle **-ne**, when attached directly to a noun, typically indicates that the speaker is female. American women tend to use "reduplicated" adjective forms (such as **itsy-bitsy** or **teeny-weeny**) more frequently than men. Russian women use more diminutive nicknames, such as **Larochka**, and **Mashen'ka**, than men do.

Professionals typically use technical language to heighten acceptance of their authority. Unless they are trying to be folksy, doctors don't say **tummy** or **belly**; instead they use the more technical word **abdomen**. People often use baby talk when speaking to children or to sweethearts. In Eastern American English, speakers of higher social status are usually called **Mister** plus last name, while lower-status persons are called by first name or last name only. In Jamaican English, the meaning of the term **supper** varies greatly according to the speaker's social class. Among the upper-middle class, **supper** is a light meal eaten between 10:30 p.m. and midnight. Among the lower-middle class, the term indicates a medium-size meal eaten between 4 and 6 p.m. However, among peasants, it is a light meal eaten between 7 and 8:30 p.m.

Note variations according to relative social difference. In many societies, it is essential that participants in a conversation adjust their language to reflect their relative social status. In Javanese, it is impossible to speak to someone without indicating a judgment of relative status. So Javanese adjust their speech to a variety of social variables, including the relative status of the hearer. To illustrate how much variation there can be, here are two versions of the Javanese question, "Are you going to eat rice and cassava now?"

High form: Menapa	spandjenengan	bade	dahar	sekul	kalijan
Low form: apa	kowé	arép	n̄angan	sega	lan

kaspé samenika?
kaspé saiki?

Similarly, in Japanese it is difficult to ask questions such as "Will you go?" without using forms that normally indicate the kind and degree of social distance between the speaker and the addressee. When Japanese business people meet for the first time, they exchange business cards that give strong clues to social status. During an initial bow participants glance at the card, assess the relative status of their conversational partner, and decide on the appropriate amount of respect needed in their speech.

Note variations according to social situation and setting. We often adjust our language to fit the occasion. For example, when giving a speech or socializing with strangers, we tend to use more formal language than when we are sitting and drinking with friends. We try to avoid swear words and use words such as **powder room** rather than **toilet** or **john**. We greet a group of friends with **Hi, guys! Hi, there!** or **Greetings!** On the other hand, we open an address to a distinguished gathering with **Ladies and Gentlemen!**

Note Nonverbal Communication

Many misunderstandings in cross-cultural communication are due not only to language problems but also to ignorance of nonverbal cues.

Learning a language is only the first step in beginning to communicate with persons from different cultures. In all societies, how you move your body or the expressions on your face are usually important parts of any message. Here are some movements that may communicate as much or more information than words:

Eye contact. In some societies, among them the United States, one shows respect for conversational partners by looking them in the eye from time to time. Not to do so may be interpreted as a sign of disrespect, lack of interest, or even untrustworthiness. In many Asian societies and among Native Americans, however, looking someone in the eye, especially a superior, is considered very disrespectful. A junior person must always keep eyes cast downward when speaking to elders or superiors.

Smiling. The timing of a smile also carries a message. Rules for when to smile vary greatly from society to society. Americans smile at strangers to signal friendliness and politeness. In much of Asia and Eastern Europe, however, smiles are reserved for friends and intimates, and smiling at strangers signifies sexual invitation, intrusiveness, or simple mindedness. Hence, Americans may appear superficial or impolite to Asians and Eastern Europeans, who in turn seem hostile, sullen, and unfriendly to Americans. In some societies, it is important to cover your mouth when smiling or laughing. This looks silly to many Americans.

Kissing. Russian men find it quite normal to kiss each other under emotional circumstances. Even Russian dignitaries have been known to kiss officials from other countries during solemn occasions, such as the signing of a treaty. In the United States, however, only women are allowed such public display of emotion. Arabs meet visiting dignitaries by hugging them and kissing them on the cheek. A nervous, jittery reaction from a visitor would hurt local sensibilities. In Japan, neither men nor women are allowed to kiss in public—one is supposed to keep one's emotions quite private.

Handing and handling. In Islamic cultures, the right hand (often called the "sweet one") is used for eating, while the left is used for bathroom functions only. Nothing is more insulting than to be handed an object with the left hand. Asians and Africans are taught to use both hands when giving an object to another person or when receiving an object. The casual American way of using either hand is seen as rude.

Pointing. Whereas pointing with the index finger is common in the United States, in Java it is considered very rude to point with anything but the thumb. In some societies, pointing is done with other parts of the body, such as the lower lip or the head.

Posture. In Asian countries, posture is a strong indicator of respect. One does not cross feet or legs in the presence of superiors. It is also important to remain physically lower than a respected person. Thus, a Thai, upon seeing an older woman, may show his respect by sitting down in the only available chair. Also, showing the bottom of one's feet is very disrespectful. Hence, Americans who put their feet up in front of Thai friends would be considered ill-mannered.

   Touching. The rules governing how and when to touch another person vary greatly and are emotionally charged. In the United States, it is common for members of the opposite sex to hold hands if they are romantically involved, but members of the same sex never hold hands unless they, too, are romantically involved. In contrast, in Asia members of the opposite sex never touch in public, since this would be considered immodest or a sexual innuendo. On the other hand, in much of Asia, the Middle East, and Latin America, heterosexual male friends can be seen walking arm-in-arm in the streets or holding hands during a conversation. In Russia, it is common for women to hold hands in public or to walk down the street arm in arm. In Japan, however, intentional touching between most adults in public is rare—even a handshake is absent. And in Thailand, patting someone on the head, even a child, is very disrespectful.

   Bowing. In Japan, bowing at introductions and on meeting acquaintances is essential to demonstrate proper respect. No real communication can be conducted without the appropriate degree of bowing.

   Head shaking. Most cultures have ways of moving the head to signify **no**, but the techniques differ significantly. Most Europeans signify **no** by moving the head from side to side. In Bulgaria and Turkey, **no** is signified by throwing the head back and returning it to normal position.

   Gestures. While people all over the world use gestures to communicate, the number permitted and their interpretation vary widely. The same gesture can mean completely different things in different societies. For example, the American sign for **okay**, with thumb and forefinger together, may mean either **okay** or **zero** in France, but it is considered obscene in Brazil. Hand gestures for **good-bye** and **come here** have exactly opposite interpretations in the United States and Latin America. And in some parts of Asia, only children can be called by using a hand motion.

   Distance between speakers. The number of inches or feet between speakers is an important social message whose meaning varies from society to society. For example, Latin Americans usually stand closer to their conversational partners (either male or female) than do North Americans. North Americans stand close only when they wish to say something fairly intimate. Hence, Latin Americans interpret normal North American speaking distance as unfriendly, whereas North Americans see Latin American closeness as intrusive and discomforting.

   Medium of expression. There are clear cultural rules for whether a message should be typed, written, or printed. For instance, Americans are not offended by typewritten letters from their friends. However, Russians expect personal correspondence to be hand written. Rules also often dictate whether a message should be delivered in person, by phone, or through a third person.

Loudness. Cultures set different standards for level of voice loudness, which may vary between sexes and in different situations. For example, in Java, well-bred women are taught to speak very softly in public—any violation would be a breach of etiquette. In China, people at a dinner table in a restaurant will talk loudly as a sign of having a good time, whereas in middle-class America, it is generally considered impolite to raise one's voice at a restaurant.

Silence. In many societies, silence is the correct response to certain questions or requests. In the United States, if silence is the response to a request, it usually means **no**. In Britain, it is often interpreted as **maybe**. But in Iran, if a woman responds with silence to an offer of a marriage partner, it means **yes**. Among some Native Americans, long silences are common when social situations are unclear. A Navaho who wants to find out more about someone may fall silent in order to do so. Most Westerners interpret such silences as lack of comprehension and will either repeat or elaborate on what they have said. In addition, silence in Navaho may also mean **no**, and this, too, may be misinterpreted.

Conversational overlap. In Eastern Europe, a person may start speaking either before the other person has finished talking or begin to speak as soon as the other person has stopped. In most parts of the United States, however, people wait for a brief moment to make sure that their partner has finished speaking. As a result, Americans in Eastern Europe have the impression that they are being interrupted or not given a chance to finish speaking. Californians have the same impression of New Yorkers.

Turn taking. Rules for taking turns in conversations vary from culture to culture as well. Japanese usually take short turns and yield the floor to their conversation partner as soon as they finished speaking. On the other hand, East Europeans tend to take longer turns and do not yield the floor unless pressed to do so by their conversational partner. In the United States, such behavior is considered to be boorish.

Thus, to communicate effectively you need to know more than grammar, vocabulary, and how to make sentences. Knowing when *not* to speak may be just as important as knowing *what* to say. You need to be sensitive to the ways intentions are expressed, interpreted, and negotiated; to the interplay between referential and social meaning; to language variation according to social and regional boundaries; and to the role of nonverbal behavior.

All this may seem like a lot to keep in mind, and it is. We have presented this information to illustrate that language cannot be approached mechanically and in isolation. Rather, it must be learned as it is used in social settings so that you can accomplish social purposes. While customs may differ from language to language, most social intentions remain the same: everyone tries to show respect and save face, make requests, give instructions and information, make a point, show intimacy, accept or reject invitations, agree or disagree, take a turn in a conversation, and so forth. Every language learner needs to keep these purposes in mind and learn the socially appropriate way to express them.

Finally, it is important to bear in mind that most people make many allowances for error—at least in the beginning—so don't be afraid to try something out while noting the reaction of your listener. Through trial and error, your ability to communicate and understand will rapidly improve.

CHAPTER 6

The Nature of Language

LANGUAGE IS CREATIVE

Language is perhaps the most creative of all human inventions. Since the primary function of language is to carry meaning and since the number of meanings that people communicate to each other is infinite, language must be very efficient. This efficiency is accomplished through several features.

To meet the demands of communicating an infinite number of messages, language manufactures, so to speak, two products: individual words and combinations of words. The combinations make up sentences or parts of sentences. One can make sentences that have never been said or written before: **There is a purple horse on the living room couch smoking an apple.** Regardless of whether you believe in purple horses smoking apples in living rooms, you can easily process the sentence and will probably try to assign some meaning to it. The point is that words are units that can be used in a great variety of ways to build sentences according to the rules of the language. These rules put limits on creativity by making some products incomprehensible: **Purple there a horse apple the living an smoking is couch room on** is gibberish and cannot be processed, although the words are the same as in the previous example.

The same creativity fabricates new words out of preexisting parts: the -burger of **hamburger** can serve as a base for **fishburger** and **chicken-burger**; the -ee of **employee** serves handily in **draftee** and **escapee**; the de- of **deactivate** builds **detoxify** and **defrock**. Note that rules keep creativity in check; **defeather** is easy to understand, but **featherde** is nonsense.

Thus, creativity allows language to accommodate new meanings and messages through innovative use of existing elements, but rules limit the nature and number of possibilities. This brings us to the next feature of language—its systematic nature.

LANGUAGE IS SYSTEMATIC

Checks and Balances

Learners may eventually reach a point when they are ready to shout "One more rule and I quit! Is there no end to these rules and exceptions?" It may be hard to believe that languages actually do operate with a finite number of rules. True, it may take a long time to learn them all. But once learned, they are stored in the brain and allow speakers to generate an infinite set of messages.

Every person who knows a language possesses a set of rules that allows him or her to understand and produce sentences and to recognize whether or not a sentence is grammatical. However, not all rules are learned consciously. Often, we deduce a rule from context, so we know that something sounds right or wrong, but cannot explain why. This is the type of knowledge that native speakers possess about their own language. It is also the type of knowledge that learners can acquire in real-life informal settings.

Since language is governed by rules, learners must come to grips with the language as a system. There are rules at all levels. At the level of sounds, for instance, the rules allow for certain combinations of sounds but exclude others. This may differ from language to language. In English, **m** cannot be followed by **l** at the beginning of words, so one knows right away that **mlad** is not an English word; at the same time, **b** can be followed by **l**, so **blad** has the potential to be an actual English word.

At the word level, rules govern combinations of parts. For example, in English, the elements **-er** or **-ian** must follow the main part of the word, as in **reader** or **librarian**; placing them at the beginning of the word results in nonsense like **erread** and **ianlibrar**.

At the level of sentences, rules tell us how words can be combined. In English, the word order is usually subject-verb-object, as in **Mary drinks coffee** or **John loves Mary**. If this rule is violated, we get **Coffee drinks Mary**, which is ungrammatical and nonsensical, and **Mary loves John**, which is grammatical but which has a different meaning.

By limiting the number of possibilities in which words can be arranged in English, grammar also helps us predict what will follow when something has been missed. For example, when you hear the sentence **Mary wore a red . . . .**, you can predict that the missing word is a noun.

When you hear the sentence **The plumber . . . . the faucet,** you can guess that the missing word is a verb.

LANGUAGES ARE BOTH SIMILAR AND DIFFERENT

Languages are alike yet different, because the people who speak them are alike in their human capacities yet different in a million other ways. In the very broadest sense, all languages share some common features, yet learners can be surprised and perplexed that a new language does not express things in the same way as their native language. On the other hand, discovering the similarities between a new language and one's native language is always a relief.

Pronunciation

A new language may have the same sounds as your own language, but they may be pronounced in slightly different ways. For instance, English, French, and Spanish all have the sound **p,** but its quality differs. In English, this sound is pronounced with a slight accompanying puff of air, while in Spanish and French, the air is released gradually.

Grammar

All languages have ways of modifying nouns. In some languages, the modifier usually precedes the noun, but in others the modifier usually follows. For example, in English we say **big house,** but in Spanish, the normal sequence is **casa grande** ("house big").

English, Spanish, and Russian all have words to express existence or presence, but Russian and English have only one verb that means **to be,** while Spanish has two: **ser** and **estar.** At the same time, Russian omits the verb **to be** in the present tense, while English and Spanish do not, with the following result:

ENGLISH	RUSSIAN	SPANISH
I am a student.	Ya student. ("I student.")	Soy estudiante. ("Am student.")
I am here.	Ya tut. ("I here.")	Estoy aqui. ("Am here.")

Vocabulary

Words in our own language come to us so automatically that we rarely think of their relationship to the reality that they designate. For instance, the English verb **to know** seems so simple and natural to us that we may assume that all languages treat the concept of knowing in the same way. Yet many languages distinguish between two different kinds of knowing: recognizing people and things, and knowing *about* something—for example, Spanish **conocer** and **saber**, German **kennen** and **wissen**, French **connaître** and **savoir**. In Chinese, there are three: **rènshi** ("to know/recognize someone"), **zhīdao** ("to know about something"), and **huì** ("to know how to do something").

Another interesting example is the English word **hot**, which refers to the temperature of the air, as in **hot weather**; temperatures of various substances, such as **hot coffee**; and degree of spiciness of foods, such as **hot peppers**. In Russian, a different word for **hot** would be used in each situation, and in Chinese two would be used (temperature vs. spiciness). It is not surprising that both Russians and Chinese would think that the English phrase **hot soup** was very unclear.

	ENGLISH	CHINESE	RUSSIAN
weather	hot	rè	zharkiy
soup	hot	rè	gor'achiy
pepper	hot	là	ostriy

Idioms

Some of the most fascinating examples of similarities and differences between languages are found in idioms and set expressions. Language learners are often surprised when a rather unusual expression has a word-for-word equivalent in another language. Just as often, they may be surprised to find that an expression does not have an equivalent in another language or that the equivalent differs in some ways.

Here are some expressions that rather unexpectedly have very similar equivalents in English, Spanish, and Russian—three languages that, although related, are quite far apart in most ways: English **to shed crocodile tears**, Russian **lit' krokodilovy slyozy**; English to **hit the ceiling**, Spanish **tomar el cielo con las manos** ("to take the sky in one's hands"); English **to know something inside out**, Russian znat' vdol' i poperyok ("to know something lengthwise and crosswise"); English **to have nine lives**, Spanish **tener siete vidas** ("to have seven lives"), Russian **dvuzhil'niy** ("one with two lives"); English **when in Rome do as the Romans do**, Russian **v Tulu so svoim samovarom ne ezdyat** ("don't go to Tula [a city famous for its samovars] with your own samovar").

On the other hand, there are no equivalents in English for the Spanish **cara de viernes** ("Friday face," or a "thin, wan face"), **decir cuatro verdades** ("to tell four truths," or "to speak one's mind freely"), or

saber más que las culebras ("to know more than the snakes," or "to be cunning"). At the same time, no language seems to have a word for word equivalent for the English expression **to go bananas**.

It is important that you have some notion of the nature of language, since that knowledge will help you in your language study. Knowing that the number of rules of a language are finite will make this task seem less imposing. Using what you know about language will mean that there is less to learn. Recognizing that language is creative should help approach the task as a challenge that is open-ended rather than finite. Learning a language is a complex but well-defined undertaking that is defined by the rules of a language and by the similarities that languages may share.

CHAPTER 7

Language Learning Resources

LANGUAGE TEACHERS

The Role of the Teacher

The beginning stages of language learning usually take place in the classroom and are thus molded by the teacher, who determines the textbook and the method, sets the pace, and creates the classroom atmosphere. However, remember that without your active input and participation, even the most outstanding teacher will not be as much help to you as he or she could. Thus it is a good idea to discuss your goals and preferred ways of learning with the teacher.

Your teacher not only models the language you are studying, he or she is also an important source of information about how the language is structured, what words, phrases, and expressions mean, and when they should be used. Check your understanding of the language by asking the teacher if it is correct; ask him or her for additional explanations if you find the explanations in the textbook confusing or inadequate. Make sure that you understand the corrections in your speech, homework, compositions, and tests. Ask your teacher to provide you with written comments on your compositions. Check with your teacher periodically about your progress.

Your teacher should also be able to provide advice on how to study a foreign language. See if his or her suggestions work for you. If they don't, try to develop your own study techniques or continue using those that have worked for you in the past.

The teacher also helps set the pace of your learning. If you have trouble keeping up, try to improve your study skills and seek extra help. If you find the pace too slow, ask your teacher for additional materials to reinforce and extend the basic information. For instance, you can do some additional reading or watch foreign language videos.

Your teacher is also an important source of motivation. By rewarding your progress, your teacher can encourage you toward greater achievement. If your teacher is not a good motivator, try to switch teachers, if possible. If not, find other sources of motivation.

Some students are self-conscious and find it difficult to talk in front of their teacher because they fear criticism. Instead, they find it easier to communicate with other students or with native speakers who are not teachers. If you feel that way, make sure that you get additional practice outside of class. Also, let your teacher know how you feel.

In many instances, a language course is taught by a teacher who is not a native speaker. He or she may speak the foreign language with an accent. Many excellent language teachers recognize this limitation in themselves and supplement the course with tape recordings of native speakers. In fact, students' pronunciation is not affected by whether or not their teachers are native speakers. The important factor is your ability to mimic and your motivation to improve your pronunciation, given exposure to native speech. Thus, if your teacher is not a native speaker, either listen to recordings of native speakers or seek opportunities to practice with native speakers outside the classroom.

LANGUAGE TEXTBOOKS

Textbooks Differ in Their Philosophy

A foreign language textbook is designed to provide graded input, activities for practicing language skills, and explanations about how the language works. Different textbooks reflect different approaches to language teaching and learning. As a rule, older textbooks were built around presentation of grammar with some reading and translation exercises. The textbooks of the 1950s and 1960s usually focused on memorizing dialogues and performing a lot of highly repetitive grammar drills. In the 1970s, textbooks became somewhat more eclectic, combining elements of several different approaches. Textbooks used today are generally written with the development of communicative skills in mind. They emphasize the ability to use language in a variety of real-life situations. Modern textbooks, particularly in the more commonly taught languages (French, Spanish, German) tend to come in sets that include a main textbook, a student workbook, tapes, videos, and even computer-aided exercises. These sets are likely to contain materials designed to develop all four language skills: speaking, listening, reading, and writing. However, in the less commonly taught languages, textbooks are often 25 or 30 years old. And in the very uncommonly taught languages, there may not be any textbooks at all. See Appendix A for names of some of the major publishers of foreign language textbooks, and ask them to send you their catalogues. If you are planning to study a less commonly taught language, call the Center for Applied Linguistics (see Appendix B) and ask for a list of materials that are available for this language.

Be Prepared to Supplement

Whatever the textbook, it will not contain everything that will be covered in a course; neither will all its explanations strictly coincide with those of the teacher. Therefore, you should be prepared to supplement the textbook with your own notes, your teacher's handouts, and other materials. Choosing a textbook is often a rather subjective process that is usually left up to the teacher or the language department. Students rarely have any say in the matter. Hence, it is a good idea to try to make the most of any textbook. Here are some things you can do to supplement your textbook and use it in the most productive manner:

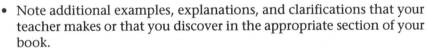

- Note additional examples, explanations, and clarifications that your teacher makes or that you discover in the appropriate section of your book.
- Most textbooks have grammar tables either in the individual sections or at the end of the book. Review these tables regularly, adding to or modifying them as your knowledge of the language grows and you discover more effective ways to organize the information about it.
- Many textbooks have a vocabulary list at the end that can be used for review or reference. Some textbooks indicate the page or lesson in which a given word occurs. This allows you to check how the word is used in context. For instance, if it is a verb, you can go back and find out which preposition or case goes with it.
- The dialogues and stories in the book provide models of how things are expressed in the foreign language. They also show how certain situations are handled—for example, how to disagree, return a compliment, or make a telephone call. They also use idiomatic expressions in appropriate contexts. Take note of these things as you prepare your oral or written assignments and borrow them from the textbook freely. That's why they were put there!
- The information in a textbook is sometimes scattered over several chapters without ever being summarized in one place. When this occurs, you should reorganize the material in your notes to make it easier to refer to and to review.

- Many language textbooks have useful appendices that may include various helpful sections: a glossary that defines all words introduced in the text in alphabetical order, conjugations of irregular verbs, tables that summarize major grammar topics, and a grammar index that indicates the page numbers on which specific grammar topics are discussed. Be sure that you know what is included in your book's appendices and how to use this information.

Your textbook is merely one printed source of information about the foreign language, albeit a very important one. As you gain confidence, go beyond your textbook to other printed matter. Try newspapers, magazines, and easy-to-read books for reading; radio and TV for listening; and a live conversation partner for speaking.

DICTIONARIES

There are Many Different Kinds of Dictionaries

Most serious language students find it helpful to buy a dictionary fairly early in their studies because it is an endless source of vocabulary enrichment. They usually buy a bilingual dictionary (e.g., English–foreign language, foreign language–English), a number of which are available for each of the more commonly taught languages. Advanced students often buy a monolingual dictionary that gives more details about the language and glosses words through synonyms and other words with a similar meaning. In some languages, monolingual dictionaries may be important even in the early stages of learning, since they provide information about declensions and conjugations, give exceptions, and show examples of how a word can be used in different contexts.

Other kinds of dictionaries can also be helpful from time to time. Among the more useful are pronunciation dictionaries, dictionaries of idiomatic phrases, dictionaries of geographic terms, or dictionaries of abbreviations. In addition, there are specialized dictionaries in such areas as sports, music, art, medicine, law, space, diplomacy, and economics. They are usually available in the reference section of good libraries.

Before investing in a dictionary, ask your teacher to recommend one that will meet your needs. Good dictionaries for the more commonly taught languages are usually available in commercial and university bookstores, especially if they were published in the United States. In the less commonly taught languages (Russian, Chinese, Japanese, Arabic), dictionaries may not be quite so easy to find since many of them are published in the countries where these languages are spoken. You may have to special order them through a good commercial or university bookstore. Finally, dictionaries for the truly uncommonly taught languages (Swahili, Urdu, Yoruba, Yakut, Slovene) may not be commercially available at all.

You will have to get them from a foreign language department at a particular university or a bookstore that specializes in foreign language books. If you are unable to locate a dictionary for the language you are studying, contact the Center for Applied Linguistics (see Appendix B).

When to Use a Dictionary?

Dictionaries offer information about the spelling, pronunciation, meaning, and alternate forms of words. When you need such information, a dictionary is a good place to start. However, avoid becoming too dependent on it. Remember that meaning can frequently be gained from context even better than from a dictionary, and often more quickly and surely. Of course, you will want to refer to a dictionary when writing , in order to find correct spellings or alternate forms. But when reading, don't get bogged down by paying too much attention to every word. Look up the most important items, if you must, but try to guess the rest (see "Strategies for Developing Reading Skills," pp. 91–99).

How to Use a Dictionary?

If you encounter a new word in a written text, you may want to look it up. Remember that some foreign alphabets have a different order and that languages that have inflections (endings) will have only one basic form in the dictionary; nouns, adjectives, and pronouns will be given in the nominative case, and verbs will be listed in the infinitive. It might take some practice to learn how to look up words. You may have to develop a number of special techniques, depending on the language you are studying. If you are a speaker of one of the European languages, you will have little difficulty learning how to use the dictionary once you have mastered the alphabet, because words are listed in alphabetical order. If, however, you happen to be studying a language that is written with characters (Chinese) or a combination of characters and a syllabary (Japanese), you will need lots of practice before you will be able to use a dictionary effectively and efficiently because these dictionaries are organized in a totally different manner.

When you look up a word in a dictionary, whether monolingual or bilingual, you may find that several equivalents are given. You must then decide which equivalent meets your needs. If you are reading, you can probably pick the right equivalent by examining the sentence or paragraph in which the word occurs. If you are still confused, look up one of the forms to see what other words are associated with it and whether they give you a clue.

If you are writing or preparing to give a talk, choose your words with care. Beware of trying to find exact equivalents. In every language, words have a range of meanings that are rarely identical. Although there may be exact equivalents, their usage in context may differ. Study the examples given in the dictionary—they should help you understand how to use the word appropriately. If necessary, consult a native speaker to verify your usage.

Dictionaries Have Limitations

Dictionaries are limited reference guides. They may serve as starting points in understanding a word or phrase, but you must add other information and observations to use them effectively. In addition, most dictionaries become partially obsolete soon after they are published because new words come into the language constantly, and dictionary makers cannot keep up with them.

REFERENCE GRAMMARS

Sometimes your basic text will not provide all the grammar information you need. Therefore, you may want to supplement it with a reference grammar. Since there are many foreign language reference grammars on the market (at least for the most commonly taught languages), you should ask your teacher to recommend one that is appropriate to your level and your needs. Keep in mind that reference grammars for the less commonly taught languages may not be available from American book publishers. They are sometimes published in the country where the language is spoken; this is the case for many languages of Eastern Europe and the former Soviet Union. Reference grammars for some truly "exotic" languages are often available only from university presses or even university language departments. If you have chosen to study such a language, you will need an instructor's help in locating a reference grammar. You can also call or write to the Center for Applied Linguistics in Washington, D.C., or the National Association of Self-Instructional Language Programs at Temple University (see Appendix B).

A reference grammar is organized by topics (usually parts of speech) so that all information on nouns, for instance, is in one place. This makes it easier to look things up. In fact, you may find it easier to look things up in a reference grammar than in your textbook if you have a question about a specific grammar point.

Occasionally, you may need more extensive explanations of the structures presented in your textbook. A reference grammar will usually provide the additional details you need. Periodically, you may find it useful to examine your reference grammar's more extended tables of declensions and conjugations to check how much you have learned and how far you have left to go. For advanced language students a reference grammar may provide examples of complex grammar constructions not included in standard textbooks. In fact, at advanced levels, a reference grammar may be the only useful source of grammar information.

Besides a reference grammar, there are other, more specialized sources of information about the language. The availability of these additional aids varies from language to language. Among them are verb wheels, vocabulary cards, declension charts, and tables of prepositions.

MEDIA MATERIALS

The technological breakthroughs of the past two decades allow you practice opportunities and increased exposure to foreign languages without your having to leave the country.

Audiotapes

Tapes and recordings provide students with opportunities for additional practice on their own terms. Good tapes especially prepared for a course not only allow students to review what has been covered in class, but frequently contain additional exercises that can improve grammatical accuracy and quality of pronunciation, increase fluency, and develop listening comprehension. Tapes can provide individualized practice with as many repetitions as needed. They are endlessly patient, available at any time, and never critical.

Tapes can be used almost anywhere and anytime. The language laboratory is, of course, a good place for using tapes because the equipment allows you to hear yourself and to compare your utterances to the correct ones on tape. This is especially useful when you are doing pronunciation or grammar drills. But if your lab's hours are inconvenient, then you can always find another time and place for listening to tapes. That is why a set of cassettes and a portable tape recorder or a recorder in your car can become as indispensable as a textbook and a dictionary. Fortunately, most language labs have high-speed tape duplicators and will make copies of tapes for you if you bring blank cassettes.

The following are some of the specific uses of audiotapes:

For practicing pronunciation. When beginning to study a new language, you can use tapes to practice pronunciation. Learning to pronounce new sounds takes much individualized practice, and time isn't always available in class. Tapes are especially helpful when you feel shy or uncomfortable about practicing new sounds and intonation patterns in front of others. Fortunately, most modern language textbooks, at least in the commonly taught languages, come with a set of tapes that include pronunciation practice. When practicing pronunciation with tapes, remember the feedback you got from your teacher and try to incorporate suggestions about how to form certain sounds into your pronunciation practice.

For learning dialogues. Listening to taped dialogues can ease the task of memorization. When you can simultaneously see a text and hear it on tape, you can improve both your retention and your pronunciation.

For practicing grammar. Taped grammar exercises can also provide many hours of useful practice. Because they offer instant feedback in the form of correct answers, they facilitate learning and retention. In addition, taped grammar exercises can be used selectively. You can concentrate on the items that give you trouble and skip the ones you already know. As Chapter 11 points out, you should always strive for 100% accuracy when doing grammar drills, because 100% today will turn into 75% or less tomorrow.

For improving listening comprehension. Tapes are often very helpful for improving listening comprehension. Many modern language textbooks include listening comprehension materials in the form of recorded passages (dialogues, news reports, stories, short lectures, etc.) that are accompanied by exercises. If your textbook does not contain such materials, try to find them. The best thing to do is ask your instructor or check the holdings at your language lab or media center. Follow the suggestions on pages 85–90, but remember that tapes can never replace real-life face-to-face communication devoted to getting meaning across.

Videotapes

Videotapes are another very important way to practice your listening comprehension and to improve your language in general. Most learners find them interesting and motivating because they show members of the foreign culture in a culturally authentic setting. Action-based dramas and conversations are especially helpful in improving your listening comprehension because they allow you to use your background knowledge to establish a framework that will help you focus your attention. Videotapes are also important because learners in a classroom get accustomed to the accent, and tone of voice of only one person. In real life, you will need to be able to understand the accents and tone of voice of males and females, young and old, as well as people from different regions of a country. In addition, teachers usually simplify their speech and are available to respond to your questions for clarification. With a video, the speakers usually do not simplify their speech and are not available to clarify things for you. This will challenge you to improve your listening while at the same time allow you to use your background knowledge to get into the story. Finally, videotapes are useful because they provide opportunities to watch and listen to authentic language in an authentic setting.

Selecting videotapes. Many textbooks in the more commonly taught languages are now accompanied by one or more videotapes that supplement the materials. When these videos provide additional opportunities to hear the material presented in the lessons in new situations, they can be extremely valuable. If the text you are studying does not come with videotapes, you might consider renting a movie tape from a neighborhood ethnic store or borrowing one from an embassy. In addition, cultural organizations, that promote the language of particular countries, will lend tapes (for example Alliance Française for French, or the Goethe Institute for German). You can also videotape materials from your local foreign language channel, if your city has one. Moreover, many colleges and universities subscribe to satellite TV stations that feature newscasts from many countries of Western and Eastern Europe, Asia, the Middle East, and South America.

Your choice of videotape should include tapes in which the language is standard (regional dialects tend to be more difficult to understand) and contains relatively little slang. For beginners, dramas are often best. Tapes of news and interviews are more appropriate for intermediate and advanced learners because there is much less action, information is more densely packed, and listeners cannot rely as much on the visual clues to provide a framework for listening.

A videotape that has been subtitled in your native language is not particularly useful, if your purpose is to improve your listening comprehension, because (1) your attention will be on the written text, and (2) you will not be focusing on improving your listening since you will have the written text as a crutch. On the other hand, if your purpose is to learn to recognize vocabulary items, subtitled videotapes can be quite helpful.

Using videotapes. If you use a videotape that is part of a course, your teacher will suggest the proper length of segment for you to listen to as well as how you should approach it. However, if you select a videotape that is not part of a course, begin slowly. Students who have not heard authentic foreign language speech before can only pay attention to about a minute at a time. Listen to the segment and try to develop some strategies to make sense of it. Consider the strategies outlined in the chapter on listening comprehension (pp. 85–90), and see if these help you.

Computer-aided Instruction

A more recent technological aid for language learners is computer-aided programs. Most of them provide opportunities to practice grammar and vocabulary in a fairly mechanical fashion, relatively removed from authentic language use. However, computer programs do provide good drills for learning grammar and vocabulary. Many learners find such programs very helpful because they provide instant feedback, as opposed to workbooks that are corrected by teachers and returned a few days later. There are some computer programs that also help with writing, for instance in French, Spanish, and English. Like tape recorders, computers are endlessly patient, never tire of repetition, and don't lose their temper.

Interactive Videodisc/Multimedia

This is a very recent technological innovation for language learning, particularly for developing speaking and listening skills. It combines the advantages of videotape (authentic setting, multiple native speakers, contextually supported language) with the advantages of computer-based instruction (opportunity to work alone, individual feedback, carefully monitored progression of difficulty). Videodiscs provide a powerful means to use authentic language with the benefit of materials organized in a pedagogically sound manner. There are some 100 programs developed for 10 languages in this relatively new medium. For a list of available foreign language videodiscs, write CALICO (see Appendix B). If you do have access to such materials, you will more than likely find them both useful and enjoyable.

PART TWO

ONCE YOU BEGIN

CHAPTER 8

Take Charge of Your Learning

FIND YOUR OWN WAY

You Know Yourself Best

Remember that unless you can take charge of your own learning, you will probably not succeed in mastering the new language. You know yourself best, so you should use your self-knowledge to guide your studies, even if it means that sometimes you will have to disregard some of your teacher's approaches and the suggestions made in the textbook.

As mentioned earlier, people tend to learn in different ways. Some are very analytical and need a rule for everything. Others are more intuitive; they prefer to gather examples and imitate them. Some need lots of repetition, while others require less. In a classroom situation, the teacher cannot tailor the approach to each individual student. Therefore, you cannot always rely on your teacher to provide you with an approach that is specifically designed for **you**. You need to experiment in order to discover what works best.

So in order to master another language, you need to be personally involved. You need to play with the language to develop a feel for how it works. The language must, in some sense, become a part of you rather than remain an external mechanical system that you manipulate according to a set of instructions. Learning a language is a little like learning to ride a bicycle. One can describe rather precisely what is involved in bicycle riding, but until a learner actually gets on the bike and takes a few spills, no meaningful learning can take place.

PLAN

Set Clear Goals

You need to decide for yourself what the overall goals for your language study are. To do this, reread Chapter 3: "Clarifying Your Objectives." This will help you develop a clearer direction and will also provide you with some benchmarks to measure your performance. For the same reasons, it is helpful to set clear goals for your daily and weekly study. Follow the goals you have set for yourself, even if this means supplementing the work that is done in your course. For instance, if your goal is to have a good accent, you can work independently on your pronunciation if it is not stressed in your course.

Establish a Regular Schedule

Language is learned in small bits, so try to establish a regular schedule for studying and then stick to it. You achieve little by occasional cramming; after all, you didn't learn your native language all at once. In fact, it took you quite a while to master all its intricacies, so give yourself the same chance when learning a new language. Do some studying every day, even on weekends and when there is no homework assignment. Work through your exercises as they are assigned, rather than do them at the last possible minute. Exercises do little good if they don't have time to sink in. Finally, find the best time of day to do your studying. Don't do it when you have many other things on your mind or when you are exhausted. Your mind has to be receptive for learning to take place.

Plan to Learn Something New Every Day

Set up a schedule for learning something new every day in addition to your classroom assignments. This is particularly true of vocabulary: you need to build up your vocabulary on your own. A good idea is to learn several new words every day besides those included in your lessons. Try color words one day, vegetables the next, occupations the third day, and so forth. Supplement the vocabulary in your textbook. For instance, if it gives the word for **dry**, learn the word for **wet** as well. Pretty soon you will impress everyone, including yourself, with the size of your vocabulary.

Assess the Difficulty of Each Task

In order to know how much effort you will need to put into accomplishing the day's assignment, you need to look it over and determine how difficult it is and then adjust your study time. In the process of recognizing the degree of difficulty, you may also come to realize what information you will need to complete the assignment. Thus, you will need to allow for enough time to find that information. Research shows that people usually underestimate the amount of time it will take them to memorize a list of words so if you have to memorize something, build in some extra time.

MONITOR AND EVALUATE

Pay Attention to Your Learning Successes

As you proceed in your learning, notice your successes and especially note what you **did** to achieve these successes. For example, when learning vocabulary, did you notice that pronouncing words out loud helped you remember them better than reading them silently? Or, when you were learning grammar, did you retain a construction better when you did specially designed exercises (for instance, filling in blanks or changing word forms), or when you were required to use the construction in order to communicate something meaningful in speaking or writing? Determine which exercises seem to help you most and for which kind of tasks: translations, mechanical drills, answering questions, compositions, and so forth. Also, note whether you find written or oral exercises more helpful and whether you retain a rule better when it is given to you before practice or when you deduce your own rule from examples presented to you.

Pay Attention to the Learning Successes of Others

Ask other students how they got the right answers or how they successfully learned something, and then see if their strategies will also work for you. For example, if someone guessed a word that you did not recognize, ask how he or she did it. Sometimes it is helpful to look at how others organize their notes, rules, and vocabulary lists as well. You can also ask other students how they go about preparing for class.

Experiment to Determine Your Modality Preference

Experiment to see if some tasks are better accomplished by using the *eye*, while others are better accomplished with the *ear*. For example, you may find that listening to tapes helps you improve your oral comprehension and memorize dialogues, but you may retain vocabulary better if you use flash cards. Remember that applying the same strategy to all tasks will not work. If you tend to rely too much on the eye, as many adults do, you may be doing yourself a disservice if you try to do all tasks through the visual modality because so much of language requires learners to use their hearing. You may need to consciously work on strengthening your aural skills.

Notice which Strategies Work and Which Don't

As you proceed with your learning, you should be on the lookout for what works and what doesn't. Once you have identified the strategies that work best for you, continue to use them. At the same time, be on the lookout for strategies that aren't effective. For instance, if you "choke up" in class when performing a dialogue with another student, could it be that you prepared for this task by reading and rereading the dialogue by yourself? If this strategy doesn't work, try working with a classmate. After all, it takes two to talk.

Experiment and Note Reactions

As you try to develop your language skills, you will have to experiment. The best test of whether your hunch is a valid one is to observe the reaction of your teacher or a native speaker. Did they look confused, laugh, or correct you? That will tell you whether you need to revise your hypothesis. For example, when using a new idiom, be sure to watch for the listener's reaction. If the listener asks for clarification or looks bewildered, you have probably used the expression inappropriately. Of course, the only way you will learn to use it is by experimenting with it until you find its limits.

The same is true when you experiment with new ways of using words. For instance, if you have learned a verb in one situation, try to use it in another. If you have learned that in Chinese one uses the verb **kāi** (literally "to open," i.e.,"to turn on") with respect to lights, try to use the same verb with other appliances. Watch for the listener's reaction; if the new phrase turns out to be unacceptable, ask why. In any case, don't wait for the teacher to provide you with all the contexts for a word; try out new ones yourself.

When learning grammar you also need to experiment and look for feedback. Often, when people are given a grammar rule, they accept it at face value and do not try to use it creatively. However, creativity is necessary because most rules have boundaries that must be discovered in order to use the language effectively. The way to find the boundaries is to keep applying the rule until you discover that it no longer applies. For example, in English, once you know that words ending in -*x* form their plural by adding -*es*, as in **boxes**, you can keep applying the rule until you discover that it is correct to say **fox-foxes**, but not **ox-oxes**. By pushing a rule to its limits you develop a feel for how it works. It becomes *your* rule instead of a *language* rule.

Define your problems clearly. Be on the lookout for your learning problems, and try to determine what you can do to solve them. If you keep examining this process, you will find that you will be better able to define your problems and thus better able to find solutions.

CHAPTER 9

What You Know *Can* Help You

Many people approach learning a foreign language as a totally new kind of learning task, different from any they have ever tackled. They assume that whatever they have learned in other courses or through life experiences has little bearing on learning a foreign language. Some teachers also treat their students as if they were a *tabula rasa*, or blank slate, on which the new language information will be inscribed.

The fact is that all of us possess a wealth of knowledge that can be brought to bear in learning a foreign language. Following the principle of "going from the known to the unknown," if you wisely use what you know, you can make the process of learning a foreign language more efficient and rewarding. You will feel in greater control because you can relate the new information about the language to knowledge you already have.

CULTURAL KNOWLEDGE

The most common kind of information you possess is *cultural knowledge*. Consider the following sentence: "Barcelona is currently enjoying fame as the host of the Olympic games, which will run from July 25 through August 9." A Martian might find it difficult to interpret this sentence, but you, as a world citizen, should not have too much trouble understanding it. After all, you bring a great deal of cultural knowledge to your reading. By answering the following questions you will see what kinds of knowledge you possess that help you interpret the sentence:

1. Where is Barcelona?
2. What are the Olympic Games?
3. What is the weather likely to be at this time of the year?
4. What does hosting consist of?

Knowledge of Facts

The answer to question 1 (Barcelona is a city in Spain) demonstrates your knowledge of geographic facts. This allows you to place the event in an urban setting. The answer to question 2 (the Olympic Games are a major international sports competition that dates back to ancient Greece) demonstrates your knowledge of historical facts. This allows you to predict that what follows might include a description of sports activities included in the Games. The answer to question 3 (the weather will be on the warm side since in the Northern Hemisphere July and August are summer months) can help you narrow the kinds of sports that will be featured.

Knowledge of Procedures/Rituals

The answer to question 4 (hosting consists of providing sports facilities for the games, housing for the athletes, and hotel rooms for visitors) demonstrates your knowledge of procedures or rituals. This knowledge helps you anticipate that the article will discuss these in further detail.

When you study a foreign language, you bring a knowledge of many facts and procedures that can help you make sense of what you hear or read. For instance, you know how to behave in a restaurant: how to order, what the sequence of the courses is, whether you should share your food with others, whether to tip, and how to address the waiter. This knowledge will help you make better sense of a conversation in a restaurant because you can fill in the gaps in your foreign language understanding. For instance, when the waiter approaches you and says something incomprehensible in a foreign language, you might guess that he is asking you what you would like to order.

Sociolinguistic Knowledge

This refers to your knowledge about how people usually talk and how to interpret what they say. For example, you know who usually speaks first: anyone who cares to, the most important person, or the oldest person. You also know whether it is all right to interrupt that person. These examples represent a small part of your knowledge of the ways people usually talk in your language. Of course, since there may be major differences between cultures about how to talk, you will need to use this information judiciously.

Another part of sociolinguistic knowledge is awareness of how to express your intentions and interpret what people say. In your own language, you know how to say **no** politely so you don't insult someone; how to recognize a polite but indirect refusal; how detailed an expression of gratitude needs to be, and how to determine if someone's expression of thanks was detailed enough; and how to greet people appropriately, depending on their status. When studying a foreign language, you need to find out how social purposes, such as thanking, greeting, and refusing, are accomplished. You will need to note similarities and differences in expressing these social functions between your own language and the one you are learning.

LINGUISTIC KNOWLEDGE

Semantic Knowledge

In addition to cultural knowledge, there are many kinds of linguistic knowledge that you bring to your study of a foreign language. You already have a large vocabulary in one language. In studying a foreign language you should use what you know to recognize foreign words. Many languages are historically related and share similar words, although they may be pronounced or spelled somewhat differently. For example, English and French share about half of their vocabulary. Compare English **aunt, uncle, cousin** and French **tante, oncle, cousin**. In addition to similar words due to a common parent, languages also borrow words from each other, either with or without adjustments to make them conform to their rules of pronunciation. Thus, when Japanese speakers borrow English words, they adapt the words to the Japanese sound system. As a result, English **baseball, football, sports** become **beesubooru, futtobooru, supootsu** in Japanese.

Similarities in vocabulary should be noted because they simplify your learning task. Consider, for example, English words ending in -**tion** (**information, institution, action**). In Spanish, similar words end in -**ción** (**información, institución, acción**). If you use your English vocabulary and apply this rule, you will recognize many hundreds of words in Spanish. Once in a while, however, similarities can turn out to be false. For example, in Russian, **miting** means "rally," not "meeting," and **aktual'niy** means "current," not "actual." The Portuguese word for rubber is **borracha**, but in Spanish **borracha** means "drunken woman"!

Sometimes, familiar looking words are used differently in another language. For example, in English the word **handsome** can describe both animate and inanimate objects, as in **handsome young man** and **handsome desk**. In Spanish, however, a young man is **guapo**, but a desk is **bonito**. Conversely, in English, people are tall and buildings can be either

tall or **high**, but in Russian and Chinese, there is only one word to describe height. So in using words that appear similar, be sure to look out for the context in which they appear.

If a language you have already studied has more than one equivalent for a word in your language, you may expect the same thing to happen in another language. For example, if you know that the verb **to ask** has two equivalents in Spanish (**preguntar**, "to ask a question," and **pedir**, "to ask for something"), you should not be surprised if there are two equivalent words in Russian (**sprashivat'** and **prosit'**), in French (**demander** and **prier**), and in Chinese (**wèn** and **qǐng**).

Phonological Knowledge

If you know a language other than your native one, you can also use what you know about pronunciation rules. If you have studied a language such as German, in which final consonants are "devoiced"—that is, **Hund** ("dog") is pronounced with a final **t** instead of **d**, you can apply the same rule to some other languages, such as Russian, in which the **d** of **parad**, "parade," is also pronounced as a **t**. Or if you have learned how to trill an **r** in Spanish, you can use this knowledge in Italian or any Slavic language. But watch out for variations. For instance, the trill may be longer, shorter, or differ slightly in the position of the tongue.

Grammar Knowledge

Even though you may not be able to state the formal rules of your own language, you know a great deal about its grammar. You may remember that Lewis Carroll used the word **uglify** in *Alice in Wonderland*. **Uglify** was not an English word until Carroll created it. But you recognize it as an acceptable English word. How do you know that? Well, you know that there is an adjective, **beautiful**, and that it can become a verb **beautify**. Then there is an adjective, **ugly**, and by analogy it can become a verb, **uglify**. You can apply the same process to a foreign language.

Another kind of grammar knowledge that you have is that of word order—i.e., the normal order in which words occur. That order can help you predict what is to follow or decipher what you have missed. For example, if you speak a language with a sentence structure like English and you see the sentence "**An independent judging organization will read every . . . .**" what word do you anticipate to come after **every**? Probably a noun, like **entry** or **submission**. When you study a new language, you need to start noticing if the word order is similar to your own. If it is, you won't have to learn new information about it. If it is not, then you may have to note the differences.

CONTEXTUAL KNOWLEDGE

Physical Setting

When you listen in your own language, there is a great deal you pay attention to besides the language in order to interpret what is being said. The physical setting may give you some clues as to what may be said. For example, if you are in a post office and see a man with a big package talking to a clerk, you can predict reasonably well that they are talking about where the package is being sent, what type of delivery is desired, how long it will take to get to its destination, and how much it will cost.

Gestures and Facial Expressions

These might give you further clues as to what is being said. If the man with the package looks angry and keeps pointing to his watch, it probably means that he has been waiting in line too long or that the post office hours are inconvenient.

Action and Interaction

These clues will also allow you to narrow your expectations. If you see two people at the train station embracing each other, you can guess that they are saying good bye, promising to keep in touch, or making plans about getting together again.

In trying to understand a story, conversation, or passage, it always helps to look for the main topic, mood, or setting. This comes from noticing the physical setting, the action and interaction, and gestures and facial expressions. Doing so will help you focus your attention and guess other important information. Ask yourself *where* the conversation is taking place. Is it in a store? Then there is probably talk about buying and selling. Does it take place in a restaurant? The conversation is probably about ordering food. *Who* is involved in the situation? If it is a doctor and a patient, you can assume that they are talking about health and medicine. If it is a police officer and a tourist, they may be talking about directions. Use what you know about contexts to help you narrow your expectations and guess more accurately.

TEXTUAL KNOWLEDGE

In reading and listening, information from the text itself can help you interpret what is being said or written. By considering what has already been said about the setting, the time, the characters, and the events, you can narrow down the range of things that can follow. Further, since you may not be able to understand a particular utterance by itself, you may need to consider how it relates to other utterances. For example, to ask for directions to the subway in Russian, you would say **Vy ne skazhete, gde tut metro?** ("Can you tell me where the metro is?"). The response **Ne skazhu** ("I won't tell you") may strike you as a little annoying or strange. However, a succeeding sentence, such as **Ya ne zdeshniy** ("I am not local") indicates that the intended meaning of **ne skazhu** is not really "I won't tell you" but "I can't tell you." As you can see, you need the second sentence to determine the meaning of **ne skazhu** and to keep you from misinterpreting it. Also, some words gain their meanings largely from the physical context. For example, the Chinese sentence **Yào bú yào chī fàn?** means "Do you want rice? (as opposed to noodles)" when in a restaurant or sitting at a table, while elsewhere it means "Would you like to eat?" (i.e., "Are you hungry?").

WORLD KNOWLEDGE

Certain kinds of logical processes are quite widespread and may help you make better sense of something you hear or read. Also, there are some universal scripts—ways of organizing dramatic stories that occur quite frequently—that can help you anticipate information that may be forthcoming. For example, in Western European cultures, fairy tales usually have a hero, a villain, a conflict, resolution of the conflict, and often the illustration of a moral principle.

Universal Logic

There are a number of logical relationships that turn up in many parts of the world and that can help you understand oral or written texts. Sometimes, relationships are expressed by such logic markers as **however**, **because**, and **if . . . . then**. If you see or hear the word **however**, you can expect that what follows will contrast with what was said earlier. If you encounter the word **because**, you can anticipate that what will follow will be a reason. As you can see, you can make use of logical relationships to help you understand what you are reading or hearing in both your native language and the foreign language.

Universal Scripts

A universal script is a story that turns up in many parts of the world. Recognizing that a passage contains that script can help make it more comprehensible and predictable. Here is an example. A famous professor was visiting a colleague in Indonesia, and they decided to see an epic play written in classical Javanese. Neither of them knew any Javanese, nor had they read or seen the play before. In one scene, the hero was battling a villain and managed to strike him. The villain doubled over in pain, and the hero turned to gloat about his victory with his friends. The professor said "Don't turn away. He is going to get you." And at exactly that moment, the villain struck the hero a heavy blow. The question is, how could the professor know what was going to happen next since he knew knew neither the language nor the play? The fact is that this kind of script is quite common in world literature, so the professor guessed that the same things could happen here. Universal scripts can sometimes be quite useful.

In summary, you bring a great deal of background knowledge to your language learning. If used judiciously and regularly, this knowledge can vastly improve your skill and speed when learning a new language.

CHAPTER 10

Assessment of Strategy Use

Why Assess?

To be a successful language learner you need to be in control of the way you learn by paying attention to procedures and strategies that work best for you in different language learning situations.

If you pay attention to what helps you succeed, you will be better able to set your goals *(plan)*, identify problems *(monitor)*, and find appropriate solutions *(evaluate* and *revise,* if necessary). In this way, you will become aware of your strengths and weaknesses and will be better able to take them into account in order to improve your learning.

How to Assess?

There are several ways you can develop awareness of your learning. Here are some useful ones:

- *Keep a diary.* Many people find it useful to keep track of their learning successes and problems. You can keep a diary on a regular basis to note the problems you encountered, the solutions you have attempted, whether or not they worked, and possible reasons for their success or failure. Here is a brief excerpt from the diary of a student who is studying first-year Arabic. Note how the author identified the source of her problems, noted her solution, and evaluated the results.

We went over our homework from the previous time in class; the homework consisted of questions to which we had to write plausible yes/no answers. George read us the questions, and we tried to read the answers we had put down on paper several days ago. I found this quite difficult and counterproductive, though the other students seemed to function O.K. I had trouble reading and listening at the same time. If I listened, I lost my place on the page. If I read, I answered mechanically without having understood the question. So I turned my homework paper over and just listened, creating new answers in my head or out loud if I was called upon. That worked much better. I guess the unfamiliarity of the script creates an either-or situation for me; if I'm trying to read, I can do nothing but read.

- *Talk to your fellow students.* One way to add to your learning strategy repertoire is to notice when your fellow students are successful in handling some task or assignment you found difficult. Ask them right away how they did it. Their response may provide you with a useful strategy.
- *Talk to your teacher.* Many foreign language teachers are interested in and knowledgeable about learning strategies. Your teacher may be one of them. If that is the case, he or she can give you some valuable advice about how to handle various aspects of language learning.
- *Assess yourself.* Another way to develop awareness of your learning approach is to work through the questionnaires that follow. They will help you become more familiar with your own strategies for learning.

The two questionnaires that follow will also mention some of the strategies you need to bear in mind as you begin your language study. In the next sections, you will find specific examples of how and when these strategies might be applied. Use the questionnaires to raise your awareness, and try keeping a diary to track your learning. The more aware and in control you are, the better you will be at learning a foreign language.

QUESTIONNAIRE 1
EXECUTIVE CONTROL

A. SETTING GOALS (PLANNING)

I. Indicate what you would like to be able to do when you complete your language study and how long you think it will take you to reach these goals.*

Skill	I would like to be able to do the following:	How long will it take?
In speaking		
In reading		
In listening		
In writing		

II. Use the scale below to answer questions 2–5:

    5 always   **4** usually   **3** occasionally   **2** rarely   **1** never

1. Do you set specific goals for yourself each time you sit down to study?	**5 4 3 2 1**
2. Do you clearly determine how you are going to organize your studying?	**5 4 3 2 1**
3. Do you learn best when you have control of your learning, i.e., determining **what, when,** and **how** you will learn?	**5 4 3 2 1**
4. Do you like to decide for yourself which errors to work on?	**5 4 3 2 1**
5. Do you have a pretty good idea of when you need to be very careful and when you need to deal only with the big picture and skip over the details?	**5 4 3 2 1**

> **A high score on this portion of the questionnaire (20–25) indicates that you are a good planner. A low score (5–10) indicates that you need to improve your planning skills.**

*If you don't have a clear idea of how long it might take you to reach your goals, talk to your teacher, talk to others who have studied this foreign language, or refer to Chapter 3.

B. NOTICING PROBLEMS (MONITORING)

1. In learning a foreign language, do you note when something is unclear, ambiguous, or not known to you, and then do you formulate a plan for resolving these problems?	**5 4 3 2 1**
2. When someone corrects you in a foreign language, do you attempt to understand why you made a mistake?	**5 4 3 2 1**
3. Can you recognize when a task or a class is going to be particularly difficult?	**5 4 3 2 1**

A high score on this portion of the questionnaire (10–15) indicates that you are a good monitor. A low score (below 10) indicates that you need to improve your monitoring ability.

C. SOLVING PROBLEMS (EVALUATING AND REVISING)

1. Do you ask your teacher, native speakers, or more advanced students for help when you do not understand?	**5 4 3 2 1**
2. Do you notice that some errors need immediate attention and others do not?	**5 4 3 2 1**
3. Do you keep track of errors that you usually make, look for a pattern, and decide how to correct the ones that form a pattern?	**5 4 3 2 1**
4. Do you keep track of the way you have learned something and whether it is helpful? If you find it is not, do you look for other ways to learn the material?	**5 4 3 2 1**

A high score on this portion of the questionnaire (15–20) indicates that you are a good evaluator of your learning and that you have a flexible approach to learning. A low score (less than 10) indicates that you need to improve your evaluation approaches and to develop greater flexibility in your learning strategies.

QUESTIONNAIRE 2
STRATEGIES

GRAMMAR

1. When you study grammar, do you look for a pattern or rule and refer to what you already know about this particular structure?	5 4 3 2 1
2. When you complete grammar drills, do you always strive for 100% mastery?	5 4 3 2 1
3. In studying grammar, do you use your knowledge of your own and other foreign languages to try to make sense of the new language?	5 4 3 2 1
4. Do you try to use the sentence patterns of the language you are studying?	5 4 3 2 1
5. When you don't know or can't recall a structure you need, do you use one you know or a combination of simpler structures instead?	5 4 3 2 1

A high score on this section (20–25) indicates that you have effective grammar learning strategies. A low score (less than 10) indicates that you should consider modifying your approach to learning grammar.

VOCABULARY

1. Do you try to remember words by using them in context, i.e., in a conversation or in writing?	5 4 3 2 1
2. Do you try to organize the words that you have to learn into meaningful groups?	5 4 3 2 1
3. Do you check yourself after you finished studying a list or group of words?	5 4 3 2 1
4. Do you associate new words with those you already know?	5 4 3 2 1
5. Do you periodically review vocabulary you studied earlier?	5 4 3 2 1

A high score on this section (10–25) indicates that you have effective vocabulary-learning strategies. A low score (less than 10) indicates that you should consider modifying your approach to learning new words.

SPEAKING

1. If you have a dialogue to memorize for acting out in class, do you rehearse the situation in your head to make sure you can do it?	5 4 3 2 1
2. If you have a dialogue to memorize for acting out in class, do you rehearse it with another student in your class to make sure that you can do it?	5 4 3 2 1
3. When you are in a store or restaurant in your country, do you try to imagine what you would say in the foreign language under these circumstances?	5 4 3 2 1
4. When you don't know how to say something in a foreign language, do you try to say it another way?	5 4 3 2 1
5. When you don't know how to say something in a foreign language, do you say something else instead?	5 4 3 2 1
6. When you don't know how to say something in a foreign language, do you ask your conversation partner for help?	5 4 3 2 1
7. Do you take every opportunity to practice speaking with native speakers of the language?	5 4 3 2 1

A high score on this section (25–35) indicates that you use effective strategies for practicing speaking. A low score (less than 20) indicates that you should expand your range of speaking strategies.

LISTENING

1. Do you try to guess if you don't fully understand what is being said?	5 4 3 2 1
2. Do you use your knowledge of the world in understanding a conversation, a movie, or a radio/TV broadcast?	5 4 3 2 1
3. If you don't understand, do you try to keep listening because you may get a clue as to what was meant?	5 4 3 2 1
4. When you don't understand, do you pinpoint for your conversation partner what exactly you did not understand?	5 4 3 2 1
5. When you don't understand completely, do you summarize what you have understood and ask your conversation partner for verification?	5 4 3 2 1

If you score high on this section (20–25), you are using effective strategies to improve your listening comprehension. If your score is low (less than 15) you need to work on improving your listening-comprehension techniques.

READING

1. Do you use your knowledge of the logical sequence of events in the passage to figure out unclear portions of the text?	5 4 3 2 1
2. Do you use your knowledge of the subject matter to figure out unclear portions of the text?	5 4 3 2 1
3. Do you use your knowledge of grammar to figure out unclear sentences or parts of sentences?	5 4 3 2 1
4. Do you rely on words that look similar to words in your native or any other language you know to figure out the meaning of unfamiliar words in the text?	5 4 3 2 1
5. Do you rely on context to figure out the meaning of unfamiliar words in the text?	5 4 3 2 1
6. Do you consider the context when you look up unfamiliar words in a dictionary?	5 4 3 2 1
7. Do you read the whole text first to get the big picture?	5 4 3 2 1
8. Do you ask yourself questions in order to monitor your understanding of the text?	5 4 3 2 1
9. Do you use contextual clues (title, illustrations, layout, etc.) in order to figure out what the text is about?	5 4 3 2 1

If you score high on this section (35–45), you are using effective reading strategies. If your score is low (less than 25), you should work on improving your reading techniques.

WRITING

1. Do you try to pick a topic that will allow you to use what you know rather than one that will force you to use what you don't know?	5 4 3 2 1
2. Do you develop an outline before you start writing?	5 4 3 2 1
3. Do you write a draft first and review it before turning in the final version?	5 4 3 2 1
4. Do you try to use the vocabulary and grammar you already know rather than look up most of the words in a dictionary?	5 4 3 2 1
5. Do you make sure that you have a correct model for the type of writing you are going to do, e.g., the appropriate form for an invitation or the correct form to address people?	5 4 3 2 1

If you score high on this section (20–25), you are using effective writing techniques. If your score is low (less than 15), you need to improve your writing strategies.

We hope that this chapter helped you take stock of language learning strategies that you have been using thus far in handling various tasks. In the next five chapters, we will present a systematic overview of many useful strategies that will allow you to approach language learning in an effective way.

CHAPTER 11

Vocabulary and Grammar

In Chapters 12–15, you will find many useful strategies for learning vocabulary and grammar as they apply to the skills of listening, reading, speaking, and writing. However, because vocabulary and grammar are essential for the development of all these skills, we will first present them in isolation and then return to them later when discussing their role in the contexts of listening, reading, speaking, and writing.

STRATEGIES FOR LEARNING VOCABULARY

One cannot speak, understand, read, or write a foreign language without knowing a lot of words. Therefore, vocabulary learning is at the heart of mastering a foreign language. There are two general ways in which people learn vocabulary.

Direct approach. In direct vocabulary learning, students focus their attention on learning words in lists or completing various vocabulary exercises. Most learners use this approach to learn frequently used words that are needed for survival skills in the language. The direct approach is time- and effort-consuming; therefore, it is fortunate that the number of words that are used with high frequency in this domain is limited.

Indirect approach. Direct vocabulary learning becomes impractical simply because there are just too many words to learn. Since a lot of vocabulary is learned through reading and listening, you need to adopt strategies for dealing with unfamiliar words indirectly instead of memorizing them. In indirect vocabulary learning, your attention will be focused on performing some other language task, such as conveying or trying to understand a spoken or written message. In the process, you will most likely begin to learn many new vocabulary items.

In this section, we would like to introduce you to some direct and indirect vocabulary-learning techniques that others have found to be effective. You should experiment with them and adopt any strategy that works for you.

Direct Approach

Strive for mastery. Whatever technique(s) you might be using, always work towards 100% mastery and test yourself to see if you have achieved it. This 100% on immediate recall will probably drop to 75% recall tomorrow and even lower a week later. Always check your retention right after you have studied and a few days later.

Put the words and their definitions on individual cards. Include a sample sentence that illustrates how the word may be used in context, particularly if it is a verb. Study the words in varying order. Check your retention when you have finished studying. Find out if commercial flash cards are available for the language you are studying.

Say the words aloud or write them over and over again as you study. Never work with words in the same order, because those at the beginning and end of the list will be remembered better than those in the middle.

Compose sentences with the words you are studying. Try different contexts, and check with your teacher.

Tape record the words and their definition, if you prefer to learn through the ear. Then listen to the tape as many times as you need to achieve 100% retention on a self-test.

Color-code words by parts of speech, if you prefer to learn through the eye. Remember that nouns are easier to remember than adjectives, and that adjectives, in turn, are easier to recall than verbs. Highlight words that cause you the most trouble so that you can give them extra attention. If you are working with word cards, put the cards with these words in a separate pile and review them several times.

Use Mnemonics

Mnemonics are techniques that make memorization easier by organizing individual items into patterns and linking things together. There are many kinds of mnemonic devices. You should experiment with different ones to see which work best for you. Here are some you may want to try.

Use rhyming. Items that rhyme are often easier to remember. When memorizing a list of words, see if some rhyme with each other or with other words that you know. For instance, in Russian, **nash** ("our"), **vash** ("your") and **nas** ("us"), **vas** ("you") should be learned together so that if one is named, the other one will instantly come to mind.

Use alliteration. Items that start with the same letter(s) or sound(s) may be learned together for easier recall. For instance, English question words start with the letters **wh-**, e.g., **who**, **what**. In Spanish, question words often start with **qu-**, for instance, **quién** ("who"), **qué** ("what"). Noting such similarities may help you in both memorization and recall.

Associate words with the physical world. Any mental image you can form for a word can be helpful, for a word is more easily learned if it can be associated with color, size, smell, feel, or some other physical characteristic. For instance, when trying to remember names of vegetables and fruits, you can associate some with being **red** and **round**, others with being **long** and **green**.

Associate words with their functions. Sometimes it helps to associate words with their functions. For example, when memorizing words for furniture, you can group them according to which are used for sitting, which for lying, and so on. You can also organize words by their conversational function. For example, have one list for words of greeting, another for words of parting, and a third for thanking.

Use natural word associations, such as opposites. In your own language, some words tend to be naturally associated. For example, given the word **cold** and asked for another word that instantly comes to mind, most people will mention **hot**. Word pairs like **brother-sister**, **big-small**, and **stand-lie** are automatically associated in our minds. Therefore, when learning words in a foreign language, try to form pairs so that when one is mentioned, the other instantly comes to mind.

Learn classes of words. Sometimes it is helpful to learn words by class, such as color words, days of the week, numbers from one to ten, fruits and vegetables, and professions. However, try to memorize them in several different orders so that you can retrieve any one of them easily.

Learn related words. Groups that share a common root, such as **white**, **whiten**, and **whitish**, are more easily memorized together than are groups of unrelated words. If you have a list of words to memorize, try to organize them into groups that share a common root, or try to link a new word with previously learned words that share the same root. At the same time, learn the meaning of some common prefixes and suffixes. For instance, the prefix **pre-** in English means "before", therefore, the term **to preview** means "to view before." In Russian, the verb **videt'** means "to see" and the prefix **pred-** means "before." So what does the Russian verb **predvidet'** mean?

Group words by grammatical class. It may help to organize a list of words by parts of speech: nouns, adjectives, verbs, and so on. Nouns are usually easier to memorize than adjectives; adjectives, in turn, are easier to memorize than verbs. Therefore, you may want to spend extra time on the more difficult classes of words.

Associate words with context. You can also associate a new word with the context in which it was used. Thus, when trying to remember a word, you can think of its context and the word will come back to you. In trying to remember the French word for **pancakes**, think of the time you ate pancakes in a French restaurant or a friend's home. You can also think of the dialog or text about food that you have studied.

Indirect Approach

Read a series of texts on a related topic. If you read a series of related articles, you will be exposed to vocabulary that is repeated frequently. Carry over of vocabulary from one text to another will help you recognize the words when you next see them. In addition, seeing the same words in different contexts will help you learn the range of meanings associated with these words.

Guess the meaning of words from context. In any passage, there are a few words whose meaning could be inferred from context, provided that you are willing to consider the available clues. For instance, if you ran into the word **sambar** in the sentence **They saw the antlers of a large sambar through the lush greenery of the jungle**, and you had never seen this word before, you might use the clues about the size, the antlers and the fact that it was in the jungle to guess that **sambar** is, probably, a large animal with antlers that lives in tropical forests. We will treat word attack strategies in greater detail in Chapter 13.

Break up the word into components. By breaking up words into roots, prefixes, and suffixes, learners can infer the meaning of words they have never seen before. For instance, you can understand the word **revalidator**, a word you have never seen before, because you know the meaning of the prefix **re-**, the root **-validat-**, and the suffix **-or**. In fact, 14,000 words in *Webster's Collegiate Dictionary* are made up of 20 prefixes and 14 roots! In order to be able to use the component strategy, you should be able to break up words into parts, to know the meaning of the parts, and to see a connection between the meaning of the parts and the context in which the word is used.

STRATEGIES FOR LEARNING GRAMMAR

Grammar is important because it allows you to express your thoughts and intentions in a way that is acceptable to native speakers. Sometimes, grammar mistakes can make your speaking and writing difficult to understand. An example in which grammar affects meaning directly is if you use a past tense verb instead of a future tense verb.

Be on the lookout for rules. Don't wait for someone to point out a rule; look for it yourself. Sometimes the rules that you can formulate for yourself will be more helpful than those given in your textbook or presented by the teacher, because they are organized in ways that are clearer to you. In addition, having found them yourself, you may be better able to remember and apply them.

Learn the rules. Although children acquire their first language without conscious learning of grammar rules, most adult foreign language learners need to understand the grammar rules of the language they are studying. Make sure that you understand how a particular rule works. This will reduce the amount of memorization you will have to do.

Organize. After having constructed your own grammar tables in a way that makes the most sense to you, make sure that you review them and add any new information that you may have acquired. For instance, you can make a table of verb conjugations in different tenses, noun declensions, or prepositions. Each time you learn a new word that belongs to a particular category you have set up, enter it in your table. This is especially important if the word is an exception to a rule and needs special attention.

Experiment. As mentioned in Chapter 8, people often accept a rule given to them at face value and do not try to apply it to different words or different situations. Experimenting with rules is necessary because most of them have boundaries that must be discovered to avoid mistakes. The way to find the boundaries is to keep applying a rule until you discover that it no longer works. For example, once you learn that Spanish nouns ending in -o are generally masculine and take the article **el** (**el muchacho**, "the boy") while nouns ending in -a are generally feminine and take the article **la**, (**la muchacha**, "the girl"), you can keep applying this rule until you discover exceptions such as **la mano**, "the hand" (not **el mano**), and **el programa**, "the program" (not **la programa**).

Work towards mastery when doing grammar exercises. When doing oral grammar exercises in class or in the language lab, carefully focus on the grammar. At this point, every one of the teacher's corrections or the correct responses on tape should be accurately repeated. Many students habitually listen passively to the teacher's corrections or the models on tape without repeating the correct form. This is not a good strategy since by repeating the corrected version you give yourself an opportunity to learn it. When you are working on a grammar point, strive to be 100% correct. In this way, when your attention is diverted to other considerations, you will be more likely to recall the correct form.

Avoid repeated errors. Try to understand why you consistently make a certain kind of error. Is it because you are not clear about the rule? Or is it that you have totally misunderstood the rule? Or could it be that you have not learned the rule boundaries—-that is, its exceptions. You can avoid making the same mistakes by checking the textbook, a reference grammar, or by asking your teacher for an explanation or clarification.

Note whether additional work has any effect on your performance. Sometimes extra practice—such as doing grammar drills—may not improve your speaking accuracy. However, using language in real-life situations may be very beneficial. The amount of time spent may not be as important as finding and using the type of activity that helps your learning.

Be patient. No language is grammar-free, although some languages have more complex grammatical systems than others. It is impossible to learn, much less remember all the rules in a limited period of time. It takes quite a long time before you are able to speak and write without grammatical errors. Work on your grammar diligently but patiently. One rule at a time and lots of practice and reviewing are good operating principles.

CHAPTER 12

Listening

GETTING STARTED

What is Listening Comprehension?

Listening, quite possibly, is the most important of the language skills, since people spend approximately 60% of their time listening. The most important first step in learning a foreign language is to make an effort to listen. This is much like the process you followed as a child. You listened for a long while before attempting to speak. In addition, listening will give you an opportunity to get a "feel" for the language and will help you improve your overall ability in it. If you don't learn to listen effectively, you will not be able to participate in conversations in the foreign language.

Interactive Listening

Most listening occurs in the course of conversations. This kind of listening is referred to as *interactive* because participants alternately play the role of speakers and listeners. In interactive listening, one can intervene by asking additional questions and seeking clarification, repetition, or rephrasing. If you are studying a foreign language in a classroom, you will undoubtedly have a chance to practice interactive listening in typical classroom conversations, which will help you get started in acquiring this important skill.

However, classroom listening won't be enough, since a lot of class time is dedicated to explaining grammar in your native language or performing other activities that do not involve listening. In the real world, listening occurs in many kinds of different situations and with many different speakers, sometimes under less than ideal acoustic conditions. Think of all the different people you have talked to in the last 24 hours. You will probably find that you have listened to quite a few individuals, all of whom spoke somewhat differently. Given this variety of real-world listening, you will need additional practice to prepare yourself to do the same in the foreign language.

Noninteractive Listening

There are other listening situations for which you will need to be prepared. These include instances in which you will not be able to intervene by asking questions or seeking clarification. This type of listening is called *noninteractive*. For instance, you may overhear conversations in which you have no part; listen to lectures, speeches, and radio; or watch TV, films, or live plays. Think of all the kinds of material you have listened to in the last week. You may have to learn to listen to just as many different kinds of material in the foreign language.

How to Practice Listening?

To prepare for the many kinds of real-world listening, we suggest that you embark on a listening program right from the very start. Here are a few suggestions for how you might go about it:

Listen regularly. In addition to language tapes specially prepared for your textbook or your course, make a regular effort to listen to the foreign language outside the classroom. You can engage in conversations with native speakers of the language you are studying (interactive listening) as well as listen to the radio, attend lectures, and watch TV and films in the foreign language (noninteractive listening).

Choose appropriate materials. For most people, the easiest way to start listening is in interactive face-to-face speaking situations, because you can exert some measure of control over the speaker. If you don't have that opportunity or aren't comfortable with it, find materials that were specially prepared for teaching listening comprehension. Many modern language textbooks contain materials that structure the listening tasks for you. Check if video materials at different difficulty levels are available in the language you are studying. Such materials are available in the more commonly studied languages, such as English, Spanish, and French, as well as in a number of less commonly studied languages, such as Russian, Hindi, Hebrew, Chinese, Japanese, Polish, and others.

Once you have become comfortable with face-to-face listening and/or the above materials, you can try finding your own authentic listening materials. Authentic listening materials abound in real life. They include radio and television programs, lectures, speeches, films, and plays. They range from relatively easy to quite difficult. Many universities receive foreign news broadcasts via satellite (e.g., SCOLA) and offer films and other materials on videocassettes through language labs, media centers, foreign language departments, and language clubs. In addition, foreign films are available in many larger video stores or can be purchased from distributors.

Find the right level of difficulty. If you are a beginning or intermediate learner of the language, start with video rather than audio materials, since the former provide listeners with visual support that often makes it easier to follow what is being said. Start with very short TV segments on familiar topics that are amply supported by visuals and that are spoken clearly and deliberately—for instance, ads, announcements, weather reports, interviews, or short news reports. You may also try watching longer segments, such as parts of movies with strong visual clues that will help you understand what is being said. If you are an advanced learner, you can listen to more complex materials, such as lectures, speeches, professional discussions, movies, and any program on radio or TV.

Choose materials that you will enjoy. People listen for information or entertainment; therefore, choose materials that you think will be informative or entertaining. If you do, your attention will be greater and you will probably understand more. For instance, if you are interested in sports, watch sports on TV or listen to sports reports on the media. If you enjoy comedies, watch them in the foreign language.

STRATEGIES FOR DEVELOPING LISTENING SKILLS

In this section, we list some common problems in learning to listen to a foreign language and provide some practical, strategy-based solutions. Experiment to find out which ones are most helpful to you.

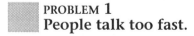 PROBLEM 1
People talk too fast.

If you feel that you cannot follow your conversational partner, try some of the following techniques, which will allow you to take charge of the situation. It is always best to specify the problem so that your conversational partner will know what to do to help you understand.

Let the speaker know that you are not following. If you don't understand a word or phrase, ask the speaker what it means. Learn how to say such phrases as "What does . . . mean?", "I don't know what . . . means," and "I don't know the word for . . ." in the foreign language.

Ask for repetition. Ask your conversational partner to repeat what he or she just said. Learn phrases such as "What did you say?" and "Please repeat" in the foreign language.

Ask your conversational partner to slow down. Ask your partner to speak more slowly. Learn how to say "Please speak more slowly" and "Could you speak more slowly, please?" in the foreign language.

Seek clarification. If you did not get part of the message, ask additional questions. For instance, if you did not follow directions, ask your conversational partner if you should turn left or right, how far you have to walk, or what the name of the street is.

Rephrase. If you are not sure that you have correctly understood what someone said, rephrase the speaker's message as best you can—for instance, "Do you mean . . .?"

Repeat. Repeat the part of a sentence you didn't understand, using a questioning intonation. For instance, if you heard a word that didn't make sense, you can repeat it. The speaker will probably then confirm or correct you.

Pay attention to intonation and tone of voice. Intonation may give you clues as to whether the utterance you heard was a statement or a question. On the other hand, tone of voice can tell you whether the speaker is pleased, angry, or happy.

Focus on question words. Every language has a limited number of question words, such as **who, what, when, where, which,** and **how.** Some languages also use "little" interrogative words that follow other words or come at the end of sentences. For instance, in Chinese, the word **ma** in the sentence **Ní hǎu ma** indicates that this is a question (literally, "You good?"). These words are extremely frequent in everyday conversations, and you should learn to recognize and use them as quickly as possible.

Assume that the <u>here</u> and <u>now</u> are relevant. Assume that what a person says is directly related to something he or she is experiencing at that very minute. Most conversations relate to the present. People commonly talk about the weather, the social setting, their feelings (which are often obvious from their facial expressions), or some action that is under way. So it is very easy to establish the topic even if you don't know much of the language. Here's an example. A teacher of the Twi language was instructing students in how to barter and bargain in an African market. In the process, she said, "I bought an X [a Twi word the students had never heard before]." At first, the class was stymied. Then they remembered that they were talking about the market and began guessing what X might be. They asked the teacher: "Is X a fruit or a vegetable?" "What color is it?" "What size is it?" They were able to identify the meaning of X by assuming that the sentence was directly related to the here and now—that is, to the subject they had just been discussing.

PROBLEM **2**
I am not getting anything out of foreign language TV and movies.

If you feel that the sound track of TV goes right by you, you should try to take control of your listening by trying to actively anticipate what you are likely to hear. The key word is *prediction*. Try some of the following prediction strategies, and decide which most help you understand.

Use visual clues. Try watching with the sound off. This will allow you to concentrate on the visuals, noticing such clues as the setting, the action, the interaction, facial expressions, and gestures. These, in turn, will help you get a general idea of what is going on. Watch the segment again with the sound on to verify if your guess was correct.

Use your background knowledge. Anticipate information in a segment by relying on your knowledge of what such a segment is likely to contain. For instance, if you are watching an interview with a violinist, you may predict that the questions will have to do with the artist's training, favorite composers, engagements, future plans, etc. If it is a commercial, then it will probably contain information about the product and its qualities. After deciding what information the segment might address, watch it the second time to find answers to these questions. This will also help you anticipate specific words/phrases that might be used.

Use information from the segment itself. What you already know about the characters, the setting, and/or the story line of an episode may help you predict what is likely to logically happen next. In turn, this will help you anticipate what is likely to be said. For example, if you are watching a drama about a warrior and he hits his opponent, what do you think will happen next?

Determine the genre of the segment. Knowing the genre of a segment will help you determine how best to approach it. For instance, if it is an interview, then concentrate on the questions. If it is a news report, a *who, when, where* strategy will work best. If it is a drama, look for the story line.

Listen to familiar elements. In listening to individual words, it may help if you first watch to determine the subject. Then your ability to hear individual words will grow. For example, if you know that a program includes a travel segment, you may find yourself recognizing the names of countries.

Listen to familiar-sounding words. Many of these are "international" words that occur in a number of languages (e.g., **capitalism**, **democracy**, **Coca-Cola**) or cognates (e.g., German **Mutter**, and Spanish **madre**). Others are words that are similar to words you already know. For instance, if you recognize Russian **brat** as **brother**, you may also recognize **bratskiy** as **brotherly**.

Listen to and jot down repeated words/phrases. Unfamiliar words or phrases may be repeated several times. Sometimes, repeated use will help you infer a word's meaning from context. At other times, repetition will allow you to remember the word or phrase long enough to ask someone what it means or to jot it down so that you can look it up in a dictionary.

Learn to recognize numbers. Think of numbers in your life and how many times a day you hear them. This will tell you how important they are in listening. Getting a telephone number and an address over the phone, a price in the store, and the temperature on the weather report are things we routinely do. Play number recognition games with a friend, e.g., using lotto or bingo numbers.

Learn to recognize proper names. Most news reports contain references to people and places. It helps to know what some "typical" first and last names of people are in the language you are studying. In addition, it helps to know what some geographical names sound like in that language. For instance, in Russian, many last names end in **-ov, -in**, or **-sky (Pavlov, Borodin, Tchaikovsky)**, while in English, many place names end in **-ton/town** or **-ville (Charleston, Youngstown, Charlottesville)**.

When listening to sports news, assume that some of the names are ones you already know. For example, if a soccer match is discussed, you may recognize the name, of Diego Maradona, a world-famous player, or if the announcer is talking about basketball, then the name of Michael Jordan may be mentioned.

 PROBLEM 3
I tend to stop listening when I hear an unfamiliar word or phrase.

Many learners, particularly in the early stages of language learning, panic and lose their concentration when they hear an unfamiliar segment. As a result, they miss portions of the passage that might have helped clarify the unfamiliar word or segment.

Concentrate on familiar elements. There is a certain degree of redundancy in almost any message; therefore, unfamiliar portions may become clear if you concentrate on those portions that you *can* follow.

Keep listening. Understanding something is better than getting nothing at all. If you continue listening, chances are that you will comprehend at least some parts of the message. It is possible that the portions you missed were not very important after all. If that is not the case, you are probably listening to something that is too difficult for you.

CHAPTER 13

Reading

GETTING STARTED

What is Reading Comprehension?

Some people think that reading is a "passive" skill, but, nothing could be further from the truth. In reality, reading is an active information-seeking process in which readers relate information in the text to what they already know. When we sit down to read, our knowledge of the language allows us to *identify* the basic forms and meanings of printed words and sentences. At the same time, our knowledge of the world in general and of the subject matter in particular allows us to *comprehend* these words and sentences by comparing them to knowledge stored in our brains. Good readers read for meaning; they do not waste time decoding each letter or each word in the text. Instead, they take in whole chunks of the text, relying on their knowledge of the language and of the subject matter to make predictions as to what is likely to follow and to interpret what is meant. For instance, in the sentence **"He has been studying wild gorillas in xxx,"** we can reasonably predict that **xxx** is probably **Africa** since it is the only place in the world where one can find wild gorillas.

As we read and our predictions get confirmed, the text makes sense to us. If our knowledge of the language is adequate and if we can relate information in the text to what we already know, we have an ideal reading situation.

When to Start Reading?

This depends on the language you are studying. If you are a speaker of English and you are studying a language such as Chinese or Japanese, it will take a long time before you can tackle real reading tasks. First, you may have to spend quite some time learning the symbols—i.e., characters or syllabaries—and only then can you begin to read real texts. In fact, it may take you several years before you can even attempt to read a newspaper. If you are studying a language such as Russian, which is written with the Cyrillic alphabet, it may take you several weeks to get accustomed to the new alphabet. If, however, you are studying French, Spanish, or Italian, you can probably start reading almost right away.

Read in the Foreign Language Regularly

As soon as you feel ready to start reading on your own, make it a habit to read something in a foreign language every day. Ten minutes a day is a good way to start. As you advance, you will find that you can increase both the quantity of pages you read and the level of difficulty of the texts.

Choose Appropriate Reading Materials

Most language learners are first introduced to written materials through their textbooks. These materials are often specially written, adapted, and simplified. Their purpose is to introduce specific grammar points and vocabulary items. These passages are usually short, written in the same genre, and glossed. They are designed to be read with attention to every grammatical and lexical detail, thereby encouraging word-for-word reading. Exclusive reliance on such texts deprives learners of opportunities to practice different types of reading strategies.

Although many newer language textbooks, particularly those for teaching English, French, and Spanish, include authentic reading materials and hints on strategy use, you will have to supplement texts provided in the textbook with authentic reading materials. "Authentic" means materials that have been written by native writers for the purpose of informing or entertaining native readers, not teaching language. Such materials are not graded to fit your level of proficiency, so you will have to select them carefully. Some suggestions on how to choose are offered below.

Find the right level of difficulty. Find something that you can read with minimal use of a dictionary. If you have to refer to a dictionary too much, you will quickly get tired and confused when trying to put all the pieces together. Fortunately, authentic texts range in difficulty from the simplest (tickets, schedules, menus) to the most complex (editorials, literary, criticism, scientific texts), so you can always find something that is appropriate for your level. If you are a beginner, look for materials specially prepared for novice readers, such as yourself. You can start by reading newspaper ads, captions under pictures, and short notices, particularly if these are visually supported. If you are an intermediate reader, you can read with partial understanding most short, uncomplicated prose in newspapers and magazines, and some simple short stories, especially if they have a clear story line. You should not worry about understanding everything. For starters, you should feel you are making progress if you can follow the main story line without concerning yourself with the details.

Choose topics with which you are familiar. Familiarity with the topic will make it easier for you to guess the meaning of unfamiliar words and to compensate for gaps in your linguistic knowledge. If you are a beginning or intermediate reader, choose short newspaper and magazine articles dealing with topics about which you have some knowledge. For instance, reading about a current event in your native language and then reading about it in the foreign language is a good way to begin reading foreign language newspapers.

Choose materials that are of interest to you. Choose materials that you think you might be interested in. If you find the materials interesting, you will be more likely to continue reading— and that is already half the battle. For example, if you are planning to travel, read a guide about the country in the foreign language. If you are interested in the country where the language you are studying is spoken, subscribe to a newspaper or a popular magazine from that country. Newspapers and magazines are particularly suited for people learning to read because they offer something for everybody, contain texts of varying levels of difficulty, and usually have photos and illustrations.

STRATEGIES FOR DEVELOPING READING SKILLS

In this section, we suggest solutions for reading problems that foreign language learners often encounter.

PROBLEM 1
There are too many unfamiliar words.

There may be a couple of reasons why you feel the text contains many unfamiliar words. You may have picked a text that is too difficult for you, and this may frustrate you if you insist on reading it. Or you may háve selected a passage that deals with a topic you know little or nothing about. Reading such a passage may require more advanced language skills. If you are a beginning or intermediate reader, it is best to pick a passage you know something about. Once you have found the right text, there are some ways to approach reading it in a more efficient manner.

Use Advance Organizers

Advance organizers are features of the text that can help you build up expectations about its content. Here are three obvious ways to use advance organizers:

   Look at titles. A title will reveal what the article is about and will help you anticipate its content. By looking at a title that says **Woman Attempts to Jump Off Bridge**, you know that the article will probably provide information about the identity of the woman, the time and location of the event, rescue efforts, etc. Then you can read the article and confirm whether your predictions were correct.

   Look   at   illustrations. Pictures, photos, and other illustrations are often used to emphasize a message. An article about a train wreck is likely to have a picture of overturned railroad cars. You can build up your expectations about the content and compensate for your imperfect knowledge of the language by using information provided in the pictures.

   Look at the format. Sometimes you can get your first overall impression of a text by looking at its general format. Right away you can tell whether it is some sort of schedule, a document, a newspaper piece, or a scholarly article. You can use this information to help you decide how you will approach the reading of the text and the kinds of information you will look for.

Use Your Background Knowledge

As you know from reading in your native language, it is always easier to read about familiar topics. This is even more true when reading in a foreign language because topic familiarity helps the nonnative reader to guess the meanings of unfamiliar words. For instance, if you are familiar with baseball, it will be easier for you to read a foreign language text about it than if you had no knowledge of the game.

Use Efficient Word Attack Strategies

Vocabulary plays an important role in reading comprehension. Since one can never learn all the words of a language, it is important to be able to recognize words you have never seen before by relying on some of the strategies described below:

Pay attention to cognates and borrowings. Many languages are related and contain the same words, although these may be spelled somewhat differently. Words in different languages that come from a common source are called **cognates**. For instance, English **mother**, Spanish **madre**, and German **Mutter** look similar because they all originated from the same Indo-European parent word. Languages also borrow words from each other, either with or without adjustments to make them conform to rules of word formation, as in the Russian verb **diktovat'** ("to dictate"). You will need to learn the regularities by which the language you are studying "converts" foreign words. For instance, Russian uses the suffix -ovat' to convert foreign verbs into Russian ones, hence **parkovat'**, **mobilizovat'**. Similarities in vocabulary should make it easier for you to read in a language that is related to your own.

However, beware of differences. Words that look the same but differ in meaning can sometimes cause problems. For example, **asistir** in Spanish does not mean "to assist," it means "to attend," and **fábrica** means "factory," not "fabric." In Russian, **magazin** means "store," not "magazine," and in German, **bekommen** means "to get," not "to become."

Sometimes the differences are more subtle, and you have to consider the context in which the similar word was used. For instance, in English, **student** means both "a person attending high school " and "a person attending a university." In Russian, **student** can only be used in the second sense.

Look for familiar elements in new words. In most languages, there are certain elements that are used for building words in fairly regular ways. If you notice how these elements are combined, it will help you recognize words you may have never seen before. For instance, in English, the element **-er** is often used to describe participants in different occupations or activities, as in **reader** and **writer**. In Korean, the word **po** means "see" and the word **po-nun-i** (see-er) means "onlooker." So what does the word **tut-nun-i** mean, if **tut** means "hear" or "listen"?

Consider the probabilities. There are certain probabilities of occurrence that help readers fill in the blanks. For instance, in the sentence **They went to the box office to get some . . .**, there is a good chance that the missing word is **tickets**.

Don't demand an exact meaning for every word. Suppose you ran into the English sentence **She bought some bananas, mangoes, and chirimoyas** and you didn't know the word **chirimoyas**. However, you could guess that it is probably some kind of fruit. Chances are that such an approximate meaning will be good enough to allow you to continue reading.

Look at the Big Picture

By considering the larger context for unfamiliar words you may be able to infer their meaning.

Read the whole sentence. Like chameleons, many words become comprehensible only in context. In English, this is true of such verbs as **to do** and **to take**. Consider the following examples: **They *did* their house *over*** ("redecorated"), **Their uncle *did* them *out* of their inheritance** ("cheated"), **The owner of the store *did* the burglar *in*** ("killed"), **She is *taking* ballet** ("studying"), **The vaccination *took*** ("was effective), **The son *took after* his father** ("resembled").

Look at the larger context. Words sometimes gain their meaning from the larger context. If you encountered the word **belt** in an auto repair manual, you would assign it a different meaning than if you saw a sign in a department store that said "Ladies' belts." Thus, if you were reading a Russian text and ran into the word **sestra**, its meaning would depend on whether it occurred in the context of family ("sister") or in a medical context ("nurse").

Keep on Reading

Look for definitions in the text. The definition of an unfamiliar word is sometimes given in the text itself. All you need is enough patience to keep on reading. Here is an example from English: **After a grueling trek in the blazing sun, they finally saw the outline of an upas in the distance.** Suppose you have never seen the word **upas** before. You can stop and look it up in the dictionary. Or you can keep on reading: **They knew that they could find shade under the dusty leaves of this desert tree.** Bingo! The writer has conveniently provided you with the needed definition that **upas** is some kind of a tree that grows in the desert.

 PROBLEM 2
I read too slowly.

One of the reasons for this is that you are probably focusing too much on each word. There are some strategies you can use to anticipate the overall meaning of a passage and hence place the words in a larger context. These will help speed up your reading. Chances are that you use a similar approach when you read in your own language. Here are the most important ones:

Identify the genre. Recognizing the genre will help you not only anticipate the information that a text might contain but also tell you how it should be read. For example, if the text is an ad, you will look for the product. On the other hand, if the text is a scientific article, you will look for the hypotheses, the method, and the results.

Approach the text as if you know something about it. It is important to anticipate what you are about to read. The more you know about the subject matter, the easier it will be for you to understand the text. Therefore, before you start reading, ask yourself what you know about the topic or situation. For instance, if the text is about elections, your knowledge of the process will help you anticipate a good deal of information in the text, and in turn, this will allow you to more easily guess the meanings of unfamiliar words. Ask yourself also about the source of the text. Knowing that an article came from a professional journal as opposed to a popular magazine will help you build up your expectations about the kind and level of information you are likely to encounter.

Read more. Like any skill, reading requires systematic practice. Put yourself on a regular schedule of reading. Regular practice will improve your ability to quickly and automatically recognize words, which, in turn, will lead to an improved reading rate.

Read silently. If you are in the habit of pronouncing every word you read, your reading rate will be quite slow. Work on forcing your eyes to move through the text silently.

PROBLEM **3**
The sentences are too long or don't make sense.

Any text, even one that is basically at your level, can contain longer sentences that you find hard to understand, even though you recognize many of the words in them. Since a sentence is not just a string of words and since the relationship among words in a sentence may hold a clue to its meaning, you need to consider how it was put together.

Pay attention to "little" words and word endings. Compare these Chinese sentences: **Tā kàn shū**, "He is reading a book," and **Tā kàn shū ma?** "Is he reading a book?" The addition of the interrogative particle **ma** turns a statement into a question. Similarly, in Japanese, the sentence **Kore wa hon desu**, "This is a book," becomes a question with the addition of **ka**, e.g., **Kore wa hon desu ka?** ("Is this a book?").

Some grammatical categories are especially important. In reading, some grammatical categories may be more important than others. For instance, learners of European languages must pay attention to verb endings in order to determine if the action took place in the past, present, or future, especially if there are no other words in the sentence to tell when an incident happened. In Spanish, for instance, the sentence **El joven *asiste* la clase de inglés** means "The young man *attends* the English class" while the sentence **El joven *asistía* la clase de inglés** means "The young man attended the English class."

Learn rules of word order. Sometimes, two sentences with the same words can have different meanings because languages differ in the way they arrange words in sentences. For instance, the most common word order in English is subject-verb-object, e.g., **Mark loves Nina.** We know that the first noun, **Mark,** is the subject because it precedes the verb. But in Russian, it is not uncommon for subjects to be at the end of the sentence, e.g., **Vchera v Moskvu pribyl amerikanskiy senator** (literally "Yesterday in Moscow arrived an American senator").

The word order in some languages can be strikingly different from the word order in your own. If your native language is English, you might find the word order of Korean so different from the one you are accustomed to that sentences may seem almost indecipherable if translated word for word into English. For instance, in English we say **Last night, I ate rice instead of bread.** But in Korean, the sentence is **Yesterday evening in rice instead of bread ate.**

Break up sentences into constituents. Regardless of the language, sentences usually consist of subjects and verbs plus such constituents as objects, time clauses, spatial clauses, and manner clauses. If you encounter a long sentence you cannot process right away, look for the subject and the verb first, and then look for the other clauses. Chances are that this will help you understand the sentence.

Learn prepositions. In most languages, there is a limited number of prepositions, i.e., words such as **on, with,** or **after.** Since prepositions are important for understanding the relationships among words and since there is a limited number of them, you should memorize the prepositions early on in your language program.

Look for discourse markers. Written passages contain words that organize groups of words and help you anticipate what comes next. Such organizers include enumerators (**first, next, for instance, for example**); chronological order markers (**now, before, after, when**); comparison (**however, yet, although, on the one hand**); cause-effect (**because, since, if . . . then, thus**); summarizers (**to make a long story short, in brief**). We call these devices "discourse markers."

You should be on the lookout for discourse markers because they will help you anticipate what might follow. For instance, if you saw the phrase **On the one hand,** you would anticipate two opposing arguments. Similarly, if you read the sentence **She took the umbrella although . . .,** you would probably anticipate something like **the forecast called for sunshine,** or **it was not raining.**

Look for words that refer to other words. Passages often contain words or phrases that refer to things that were mentioned earlier or are about to be mentioned. This is usually done with the help of pronouns or synonyms. When you run across such words, it is sometimes necessary to look back or forward in the text to check what they refer to. For instance, **People are afraid of snakes.** *They* **think that** *these creatures* **are dangerous even when** *they* **are totally harmless.** To understand these two sentences, it is important to figure out that the first **they** refers to people, whereas the second **they** refers to snakes. In addition, you have to figure out that **these creatures** refers to snakes and not to people.

CHAPTER 14

Speaking

GETTING STARTED

When to Start?

Some learners who are studying a foreign language on their own think that they should hold off speaking until they have mastered the "basic" grammar and vocabulary of the language. They feel this way because they are apprehensive about making mistakes and about not being understood. However, the truth of the matter is that the only way to learn the grammar and vocabulary of a new language is by practicing them in different contexts. So if your goal is to learn how to speak a foreign language, you should start practicing speaking as soon as possible. However, don't insist on immediate mastery.

STRATEGIES FOR DEVELOPING SPEAKING SKILLS

In this section, we list some common problems in learning to speak in a foreign language and provide some strategy-based solutions.

 PROBLEM 1
I have very poor pronunciation. Native speakers often don't understand me.

Most adults learning a foreign language tend to retain their native accent. However, there are a number of things you can do to improve your pronunciation. Experiment and see which of the following work best for you:

Imitate the rhythm and intonation of the language you are studying. If you can reproduce the rhythm and intonation accurately, other pronunciation errors (e.g., mispronouncing certain sounds) will not be so noticeable and your speech will be easier to understand.

Compare your pronunciation to the model(s) on tape. If you are using pronunciation tapes, make sure that you record yourself and keep comparing.

Listen carefully and repeat aloud after your teacher or a native speaker. Ask them to comment on your pronunciation.

Ask your teacher how certain sounds are formed. Watch what he or she does when pronouncing them. Practice the sounds at home in front of a mirror.

Practice a sound separately at first; then use it progressively in words and sentences. Try tongue-twisters involving the sound.

Make a list of words that give you pronunciation trouble, and practice them.

PROBLEM 2

I keep making the same mistakes over and over again.

Learn from your errors whenever possible. To make errors an instrument of learning, instead of a source of frustration, you must realize that the process of learning to speak a foreign language is one of successive refinement, not instant mastery. You should constantly accommodate new information to the system of rules that you have learned or have developed on your own.

Distinguish, whenever possible, between a casual slip and a recurring error. Casual slips are not serious; even native speakers have occasional slips of the tongue, and you should not worry about them. However, errors that you make consistently show that you have not mastered some aspect of the language. They require additional work.

Try to understand why you consistently make a certain kind of error. Is it because you are not clear about a rule? Or is it that you have totally misunderstood a rule and are applying a nonexistent version of it? Is it because you have not learned the boundaries of the rule—that is, its exceptions? Ask your teacher for clarification or check your textbook.

Note the relative seriousness of your errors. Not all errors are equally serious: some errors provoke stronger reactions from listeners than others. Often the mistakes that cause the most reaction are sociolinguistic ones, such as using the informal German **du** instead of the formal **Sie** to address your teacher. Even among grammatical errors, some are more serious than others. Errors such as a wrong ending are often overlooked in real communicative situations. For instance, using the Spanish present tense **voy** ("I'm going") instead of the past tense **fui** ("I went") can confuse a listener about when the action took place. On the other hand, lack of agreement between article and noun such as **un casa** instead of **una casa** ("a house") is not as serious because it doesn't affect meaning.

Accept some corrections on faith. You may need to accept corrections from your teacher or native speakers without requiring an explanation. This may happen when you are trying to use language that is above your head. Both instances may involve grammar or words that you have not yet learned or that are difficult to explain. Adopt each correction, store it, and analyze it later.

Determine how much error is tolerated in a particular language. Speakers of some languages are less tolerant of errors made by foreigners than are speakers of other languages. Commonly compared extremes are French speakers, who are very intolerant of foreigners' mistakes, and Chinese speakers, who are very permissive. When you use the new language outside of class, try to gauge the amount of error that is tolerated by native speakers of the language you are studying because it can indicate how much attention you should give to developing accuracy in speaking. At the same time, note what kinds of errors seem to most bother native speakers of the language you are studying. Do they seem to be more concerned about grammatical errors? Are they more bothered by errors in etiquette? Or are pronunciation errors a major source of irritation?

PROBLEM 3
It disturbs me when I am corrected in the middle of a sentence. It makes me lose my rhythm and forget what I was trying to say.

Sometimes, with all good intentions, a teacher constantly interrupts to correct students while they are trying to say something. When this happens, students may become intimidated, lose all interest in speaking, and fail to learn to communicate, although they may learn something about the grammar. At the same time, the teacher may wonder why all the corrections did not improve the students' speaking skills. The answer, of course, is that the students shouldn't be interrupted while they are speaking. Comments should be made later, and only the most serious errors should be corrected. Serious errors are those that cause misunderstanding or that occur repeatedly.

Negotiate with your teacher when you want errors corrected. It is a good idea to let your teacher know how you feel about having your mistakes corrected while you are speaking. Ask the teacher to discuss your mistakes after you have finished speaking rather than interrupt your train of thought. If that does not work, change teachers when you can or find native speakers outside of class to practice with. Outside of language learning situations, most native speakers focus on the message rather than on the grammatical forms used to deliver it. They will let you know when they don't understand, but will usually let you speak without interruptions.

PROBLEM **4**
I have very few opportunities to speak in the foreign language.

Language learning must be an active process. Learners who make a conscious effort to practice their foreign language and who seek out opportunities to use what they have learned are more successful than learners who assume a passive attitude and rely on the teacher to do the whole job. It is necessary to overcome inhibitions and get into situations where you must speak in the foreign language. A few tips on how this can be done follow:

Perform every classroom activity. Do every task, even if the teacher does not call on you. For example, if the teacher asks someone else a question, make up your own answer. Complete exercises in your head when it is someone else's turn, and check your answers against theirs. Listen to the other students and to the teacher's responses.

Interact with native and skilled speakers, including your teacher. Feel free to speak to your teacher outside of class. Together, you can use your new language to discuss a wide variety of topics. Also, try to find native speakers on your campus or in your neighborhood. Many colleges have international student programs or clubs that you can join. Many cities have ethnic neighborhoods with stores and restaurants. Visits to such neighborhoods will give you an opportunity to try out dialogues you have learned in class. Unlike your fellow students and teacher, a native speaker in a store or restaurant will not know the other half of the dialogue and will give you unexpected responses—and this is exactly when learning will take place.

Interact with classmates or other students in your language program. Talking with your classmates or other students taking the same language can be an easy and enjoyable way to get some practice. You may also find that you feel less inhibited about trying out new things. Many language departments have language clubs, language dorms, and language conversation tables. These usually provide an opportunity to meet other students, graduate teaching assistants, and faculty with whom you can practice your newly acquired language. They also offer cultural activities, such as informal meetings with native speakers of your new language.

If you are living in a country where the language is spoken, put yourself into situations where you will have to communicate. Make phone calls, go shopping, run errands, ask people for directions or help, and so forth. You may have to make an effort to overcome your initial inhibitions.

Best of all, make friends with people who speak the language you are studying. A sustained relationship provides the motivation to communicate and takes away the anxiety involved in speaking to strangers. Friends will also know your language level and will try to tailor their speech to your ability.

PROBLEM 5
I don't say much because I am not sure that I know how to say something correctly.

There are two things you can do. One is to prepare yourself for the various communicative situations you expect to find yourself in. The other is to accept your limitations in the foreign language and to do the best you can with what you know.

Be prepared. People who practice silently often find that it becomes a habit. Interestingly, children learning their first language frequently practice with imaginary partners, have conversations with no one in particular, and talk to objects and toys. They endlessly repeat words and sentences and make up nonsense words and phrases. Apparently these activities are an integral part of language learning for children. There is no reason why they should not also help adults.

Rehearse silently in the foreign language. The easiest way to practice is to rehearse silently, since it does not require any particular time, place, equipment, or partner. For instance, you can look at objects and try to silently name them in the foreign language, or look at persons and try to describe them in detail.

You can also prepare yourself for communicative situations you will need to handle (particularly if you are or will be living in the country where the language is spoken), for instance, to make a doctor's appointment or to place a long-distance telephone call. You can prepare by looking up key vocabulary items and finding out from native speakers how certain things are said in the language.

You can also rehearse everyday situations. For example, after you have conducted a transaction with a salesperson, clerk, or waiter in your own language, pretend that you have to do it in the foreign language. What would the same conversation have sounded like in France, Italy, or Japan? "Two croissants, please. And a cup of black coffee." "Spaghetti with marinara sauce and a bottle of Chianti, please." "Two bowls of saimin and don't forget to bring the chopsticks." Then, when you actually need to say these things in a real-life setting, you'll be ready.

Learn to live with uncertainty. When speaking, you may feel uncertain about your ability to get your message across, but don't let this stop you. Some people won't say anything unless they are sure that they can say it perfectly. However, this is a mistake, for in the beginning, you can't expect to say things perfectly. When your goal is to communicate, you should simply concentrate on producing a normal flow of speech and not be overly worried about individual items. A message spoken at the time it is needed, no matter how flawed, is worth many unspoken messages, no matter how perfect. In a communicative situation, it is better to say something promptly rather than say nothing at all or take so long to compose your message that you exhaust your listener's patience and kill interest in further communication.

Avoid the vicious circle. People who don't say anything because they are worried about making mistakes can fall into a vicious circle; they make errors because they haven't practiced enough, yet at the same time they deprive themselves of the opportunity to practice for fear of making mistakes. Remember that language learning is a gradual process that requires much practice, including making errors and being corrected. Don't hold back until that magic moment in the future when you think you will be able to speak without making errors. Without practice, that moment will never come.

PROBLEM 6
Sometimes I get stuck in the middle of a conversation and can't get myself out of trouble.

Involve your conversational partner. If you are stuck, don't get discouraged. You are not alone and there are some things that you can do.

Get help. As soon as you start studying a foreign language, you should learn how to ask such things as "How do you say that in . . .?", "Can I say . . .?", "Is it correct to say . . .?" and "What is the word for . . .?". If you don't know the word for **librarian** in the foreign language, ask **What do you call a person who works in a library?** Your partner will gladly respond, and you will be able to keep the conversation going.

Use your own resources. Use whatever you know to get your message across, even though you may suspect that there are better ways of saying it. Attempting to say something is better than saying nothing at all. In the process, you may even learn the proper way to say what you had in mind.

Paraphrase. If you don't know or if you forget the exact word you want, say it another way. For example, if you forget how to say **warm**, say **not very hot**. If you forget the word for **hat**, say **thing on top of your head**.

Use synonyms. If you have trouble remembering how to say something exactly, use a general term. For instance, if you forgot how to say **violin**, say **musical instrument**. Your listener will probably catch on.

Gamble on cognates. Historically related languages, such as French, Spanish, and Portuguese, or Russian, Polish, and Serbo-Croatian, share many words with similar meanings but somewhat different shapes.

For example, **activité** in French is **actividad** in Spanish and **actividade** in Portuguese. In Russian, the word for "people" is **lyudi**, in Polish it is **ludzie**, and in Serbo-Croatian it is **ljudi**. It is very helpful to try out cognates to keep a conversation going. Beware, though, because similarities can be misleading. For example, the English word **embarrassed** and the Spanish word **embarazada** may look similar, but they have quite different meanings. **Embarazada** means "pregnant"!

Use gestures. You can use gestures or other physical movements to express your ideas. For example, if you don't know the word for **applaud**, show your listener what you mean. This will help keep the conversation going.

Avoid problems. One way to maintain a conversation is to avoid problem areas. For example, if there are some words that you have difficulty pronouncing, avoid them by using synonyms. Or if you are unsure of how to use the subjunctive in Spanish, you may avoid trying to express possibility, doubt, and desire. This may limit what you can say, but at least you won't slow up the conversation. You have to be smart about when and how to use avoidance. When correctness is important, you may want to avoid the troublesome area and substitute something you know better. However, if communication is most important, avoidance may actually cause misunderstanding. Also, if you feel that you must always be correct, you may avoid so many situations that you won't make progress.

PROBLEM 7
I'm so slow in conversation that my conversational partner(s) usually take(s) over.

Conversation has a natural tempo, and people are not very tolerant of what they perceive to be long pauses. When you speak your own language, you usually let your conversational partner know that you haven't finished and are still thinking about what to say. The same is often true in a foreign language. There are some things that native speakers use in such situations that you can and should apply to a foreign language.

Use hesitation fillers. It helps to learn the sounds, gestures, words, or phrases that let your listener know that you are groping for a word or thought. For example, in English some common fillers are **well**, **let's see**, and **you know**. In Chinese, the phrase **nèige** ("that") is repeated several times. Note that native speakers use these expressions all the time. This will help you in two ways. First, your listener will know what you are doing and may even try to help. Second, it makes your conversation seem more natural, since we all tend to pause and think from time to time. Think of how you handle such situations in English. Then find a hesitation filler that you like in your new language.

Warn your partner. It is also helpful to let your partner know that you are groping for a word by actually saying "Just a minute, I'm trying to think."

    Buy time. You can always buy yourself some time to plan your utterance by starting out with such phrases as "This is a very interesting issue," It is a difficult question," or "Let's see now." Such phrases will help maintain the tempo of the conversation.

PROBLEM 8
I find that native speakers don't understand me at all.

There are a number of reasons why native speakers may not understand you. Your pronunciation may be very far off the mark. If so, take a look at the suggested strategies for improving pronunciation. The most common reason for not being intelligible to native speakers is overuse of translation from your native language. The meaning of a set expression or an idiom does not equal the sum of its parts. For instance, the English expression **How are you doing?** means "How are you?" Chances are that if you translated this sentence word for word into another language, you would not be understood. In Russian and Spanish it would mean "How do you make?" Another good example can be taken from Guarani, a language spoken in Paraguay. People often say **eguahęmíke?** ("Are you going to come in?") when you pass their home. What they really mean is "How are you?"

    When you are a beginner, a better strategy is to learn some ready-made chunks of language. Here are some of those you should look for:

    Learn expressions from dialogues and texts. Material you have studied in class can provide ready-made bits of language for use in real-life situations. A line memorized from a dialogue or a reading passage can pop out very quickly because you do not need to construct it yourself. Most of the time you cannot rely completely on memorized material, but you need to learn how to combine memorized pieces into phrases and sentences that express your own meanings.

    Learn idioms or expressions for future use. The meaning of an idiom or expression is often clarified by its context. Recalling the context in which you first saw or heard an idiom will help you remember and use it correctly. For example, suppose you hear one Spanish speaker saying to another when meeting, **¿Qué tal?** (literally: "What such?"), with the other answering, **Bien. ¿Y tú?** ("Well, and you?"). It should not matter too much what **tal** means in this context. The important thing is the whole utterance, the gestalt. Use the expression next time you have to greet someone. Another example is the Russian combination **Vot kak!** (literally: "Here how!") which means "Is that so?" The English word for word equivalent is obviously nonsensical. Once you find out its meaning, just treat the whole expression as one item or word. Put it away for future use to express surprise.

    When using idioms, be sure to watch for the listener's reactions. If the listener does not understand what you said or looks bewildered, you have probably used the phrase inappropriately. Of course, the only way you will learn to use it is by experimenting until you find its limits.

PROBLEM 9
I don't think native speakers enjoy talking to me in the foreign language.

Since the primary purpose of learning another language is communication, it is important to identify and learn the ways in which native speakers organize conversations and accomplish communication goals. This is what makes conversation worthwhile. Among the communication routines are ways of beginning and ending a conversation; encouraging a speaker to keep talking; apologizing; accepting and refusing an invitation; asking for directions; seeking and offering help; and expressing reactions. In any language, there are always routine ways of accomplishing these tasks. It is desirable to learn some of these routines because they show that you are involved and want to converse. Use of these formalized routines will help you maintain a conversation. However, be sure to learn the phrases that are culturally acceptable in the language you are studying. As you become more advanced, you will learn how to vary the routines to accomplish your social purposes. At the beginning, however, the basics are enough to get you through most situations. The trick is to get communication tasks accomplished with limited language skills. Some examples of formalized routines follow:

Learn some phrases for beginning and ending conversations. Every language has standard greetings, introductions, courtesies, and leave-takings. In English we begin a conversation with **Hello!** or **Hi!** and may end with **Take care, See you later, I gotta go now,** or **I'll see you.** In telephone conversations, English speakers also have clear rules for beginning and ending conversations. When making a business call, the person calling says **Hello, I would like to speak to so and so, please.** When told to hold the line, the caller will often say **thank you.** When the conversation is over, the conversational partners usually say **good-bye.** However, in Russian, formalized routines are different. A typical business call may not require greetings, thank you's, or leave-takings. Instead, **Pozovite Ivanova k telefonu** ("Call Ivanov to the phone") is a typical opening for a business call, and the conversation may end with **Vsyo!** ("That's all!") which sounds very brusque to Americans.

Learn expressions that show you are paying attention and following the conversation. In English, we use such comments as **Yeah, Good, My goodness, Uhuh, Wow, Really?, How strange, How interesting** to encourage a conversational partner. Inserting such phrases at the right times indicates that we understand and are interested. You should learn to do the same thing in the foreign language, using expressions appropriate for the culture. For example, in English, when someone is talking and a listener wants to show that he is paying attention, he will often say **I know . . . I know . . . I know . . .**, which signals interest and involvement. The counterpart in Russian is **da . . . da . . . da . . .**, which means "yes . . . yes . . . yes . . .." Saying **I know** in these circumstances in Russian would be annoying because it signals to the speaker to get on with the conversation, not that the listener is involved and interested.

Learn how to express your reactions. You should learn how to express your impressions and comment on what is going on. In English, we praise or criticize someone with phrases such as **You look nice, What a good idea!** or **How stupid of me!** Learn the appropriate ways of expressing various reactions in the language you are studying.

Also, learn how to agree and disagree. In English, we use phrases such as **I agree, Really, Certainly, You're right**, and **I don't agree**. However, rules for expressing one's reactions govern the use of particular phrases with particular persons in particular settings. For example, it would be inappropriate for subordinates to say **That was a dumb idea** to their superiors. Instead, they might ask **What do you think of that idea?**

Learn to involve your conversational partner. It is common to involve one's conversational partner by using expressions that ask for confirmation of preceding comments. In English, we use such questions as **How did you like that? What do you think of that? What's your opinion? Do you agree?** and **Don't you think so?** Use of these indicates that you are interested in your conversational partner's ideas.

Learn ways of managing a conversation. Conversation-management techniques include

- Attention getters: **Hey, Mary!**
- Politeness routines: **Thank you very much, Excuse me.**
- Suggestions: **Let's . . .**
- Requests: **Come here! Wait a minute!**

Learn some routines for refusing and accepting invitations. To avoid seeming rude, you need to learn culturally acceptable ways of refusing and accepting. For example, in Arabic cultures, refusal is often done by saying **God willing**. By saying this phrase without details, such as time and place, you have refused an invitation. If you say **God willing** and give details, you have accepted. English formulas for accepting include phrases such as **I'd love to, How nice of you to invite me**, and **I'll be there.**

CHAPTER **15**

Writing

GETTING STARTED

Writing in One's Own Language

It is probably fair to say that there is no such thing as a native writer. Writing is a difficult skill, even in one's language. If you are a good writer, you will probably be a good writer in a foreign language once your language proficiency allows you to deal with ideas freely. Most learners find that strategies which helped them achieve better results when writing in their own language can also be applied to foreign language writing.

What do People Write?

In your own language, you may use writing for a wide variety of situations. Make a list of all the kinds of things you have written in your own language during the last month. It should give you some indication of what your writing needs are in your own language, although it is not unreasonable to expect that some needs will be different in a foreign language. Most people engage in such everyday writing tasks as filling out forms, taking down telephone messages, and writing simple notes; some people may also have to handle private and/or business correspondence; finally, some individuals need to be able to write complicated prose such as technical reports, articles, and even books. However, chances are that you may not have to do all this writing in the language you are studying. Since learning to write well is extremely time consuming, it is helpful to have a good idea of what your writing needs in the foreign language will be so that you can focus your efforts.

Different Writing Systems

If you are studying a language that has a writing system similar to your own (e.g., you are an English speaker learning Spanish), you may be able to start writing simple words and even short sentences almost right away, and once you have learned the spelling rules of the new language, you should be able to write down most of the words and sentences you have learned. It might take you a bit longer if the alphabet contains a few unfamiliar letters or familiar letters that stand for different sounds. This can happen when speakers of a Western European language study an Eastern European language. For instance, if they are studying Czech, they will have to learn that the unfamiliar-looking letter č stands for the sound [ch], while the familiar letter c represents the sound [ts].

Things can be further complicated when you are trying to learn a language written with an alphabet that has many unfamiliar letters. For instance, this would be the case if you were a speaker of a Western European language who is studying Russian or Greek. You would have to learn that the letter Λ stands for [l] and that the letter Π stands for [p] in both languages. It would, probably, take you a couple of weeks to become comfortable with this type of new alphabet but less, however, than if you were learning an alphabet that was radically different from your own. This is the case with Hindi/Urdu, Hebrew, and Arabic, where you would have to learn to write not only entirely unfamiliar letters but also learn to deal with radically different spelling patterns, such as leaving out vowels in Hebrew and Arabic.

Finally, if you have chosen to study Chinese, you will need lots of time because each word is written with a unique character or unique combination of characters. Therefore, you will need to learn many thousands of characters to become literate, and most learners of Chinese find that even after a couple of years of language study they can handle only the very simplest writing tasks. Japanese is even more complicated because in addition to characters, there are also special symbols for grammatical words (particles, tenses, etc.).

Speaking vs. Writing

In speaking, especially in casual conversations, people tend to use short sentences. It's usually all right to leave sentences unfinished, to omit parts of sentences, to use a lot of pronouns and words like **this** or **that**, to point at things, and to use gestures, because the listener is right there and can always ask for clarification if he or she doesn't understand. In contrast to the speaker, the writer has to make his or her ideas clear to the readers, because they are separated from the writer by time and space. For this reason, the writer has to be much more explicit and clear. In addition, writing conventions in many languages, such as English, German, Russian, and French, require longer sentences and more refined vocabulary than are normally used in speaking.

Some languages make an even greater distinction between the spoken and the written language. For instance, the Chinese use colloquial forms of the language when speaking. In writing, however, they use many forms taken from Classical Chinese—a language that is not spoken and that exists only in written form. Learners of Chinese who wish to learn how to write sophisticated prose will need to study Classical Chinese in addition to modern colloquial Mandarin. The situation is similar in Arabic.

Writing to Learn the Language vs. Learning to Communicate in Writing

If you are studying a foreign language in a formal setting, you will probably do a great many written exercises to practice grammar and vocabulary, especially in the beginning. However, you must realize that this type of writing is designed to help you learn the language and that it does not have a counterpart in the real world. This means that in addition to written exercises, you will need to learn how to communicate real-world messages in the foreign language. In turn, this means that you will have to learn how to observe culturally required writing conventions, such as appropriate ways of inviting people, turning down invitations, requesting information, and congratulating. Writing is in part culturally determined, and reader expectations are culturally bound as well. As a result, one can offend a native speaker with one's perfectly grammatical note by simply addressing him or her in the wrong way.

Accuracy is Important

Errors often occur in speech because of pressure to respond quickly. Speaking involves many things simultaneously: choosing meaning, correct grammar, appropriate vocabulary, and proper pronunciation. Since meaning is most important, a speaker often concentrates on it and may let other aspects slip. This is natural, and as a result you are likely to make a lot more errors in speaking than in writing. Fortunately, listeners are much more tolerant than readers. Listeners don't have the time to analyze every mistake you may make, but readers do. Therefore, when writing, give extra care to correctness. Everything you write, from a simple note to a business letter, must be your best possible effort and as error-free as you can make it.

+ Exchange e-mails with colleague.

Write Regularly in the Foreign Language

Writing is a good way to practice what you already know while learning how to compose themes in a foreign language. Find your own reason for writing if your teacher does not give writing assignments on a regular basis. A pen pal can provide good motivation. You will learn a lot by trying to communicate with someone who shares your interests but comes from another culture. Corresponding with a pen pal abroad is sometimes possible via computer networks. Find out if your institution has access to such a network. Another good way to maintain a regular writing schedule is keeping a diary in a foreign language.

STRATEGIES FOR DEVELOPING WRITING SKILLS

In this section, we list some common problems in learning to write in a foreign language and provide some practical, strategy-based solutions.

PROBLEM 1
I can't see my own mistakes.

Have someone else look at your writing. Many people do not see their own mistakes. Therefore, it is a good idea to get another pair of eyes to look over what you have written. Ideally, one can ask a native speaker to check one's writing, but native speakers are not always available. Peer editing, or exchanging papers with another student, can be helpful although sometimes not completely reliable.

PROBLEM 2
Sometimes people do not understand what I have written.

There may be several reasons why this problem arises. In the first place, your strategy may be to compose a sentence in your native language and then translate it word for word into the target language. In turn, this may lead to excessive reliance on the dictionary, which can be time-consuming and frustrating, with the result that you are not understood. Here are a few tips to avoid the literal translation trap.

Use what you know. Use familiar words, phrases, and sentence patterns you have learned or seen in target language texts. They are more likely to be understood since they are correct and probably resemble what native speakers might have written under the circumstances.

Avoid excessive reliance on the dictionary. If you have to look up a half-dozen words to write a ten-word sentence, there is a high probability that the sentence will not be comprehensible to native readers, not even those used to dealing with learners of their language, such as your instructor. Every time you look up a word in a dictionary, you run the risk of picking the wrong one, especially if it is a verb with many meanings (see Chapter 14, "Speaking").

Imitate. Imitate native speakers' writing. For instance, in writing a response to a personal note, look at the format, the ways in which the writer of the note addressed you, how he or she started and ended the note, etc. This will make your writing more understandable than if you were to translate from your own language.

Plan before writing. People's writing is sometimes difficult to understand even when they are writing in their own language because what they have written is disorganized and sentences do not relate logically to each other. A successful text is one in which sentences build meaning in relation to each other and the overall topic. Therefore, you should consider the function of each sentence in light of its relation to the main topic in order to provide readers with a clear sense of purpose.

Revise. Writing does not begin or end with one draft. Revise at all levels (lexical, phrasal, sentential, discoursal). Rewrites in and of themselves usually improve content.

PROBLEM 3
My grammar is terrible. What can I do?

As mentioned earlier, people are quite intolerant of written errors, so your writing should be as free of grammar mistakes as possible. In fact, you won't be able to communicate in writing unless you learn the grammar of the language. Here are a few tips:

Check your grammar. Sometimes, grammar mistakes can make your writing difficult to understand, e.g., if you use past tense instead of future. Have a grammar reference handy when you sit down to write something in the foreign language; then review what you have written for grammatical accuracy. Check with someone if you are not sure.

Enlist your teacher's cooperation. Establish a channel of communication with your teacher regarding writing and teacher's comments by asking for feedback on grammar and other errors. In that way, you should be able to correct your own writing and avoid repeating the same mistakes. At the same time, try to understand the principle(s) behind the teacher's comments about your writing.

PROBLEM 4
I have the worst time spelling words in the foreign language.

There may be several reasons for this. If you are a good speller in your own language but have trouble with foreign language orthography, think of all the things you did that made you a good speller and apply them to the language you are studying. If, however, you have trouble spelling in your native language, then you might try some of the following strategies:

Look for regular patterns in spelling. Look for regular sound-letter correspondences. For instance, in Russian, the sound [a] can be represented either by the letter **a** or the letter **o**, as in p**a**rad ("parade") and M**o**skva ("Moscow"). Find out whether there are any rules that would tell you when to write **a** or **o**. If there is a rule, remember it and apply it when in doubt. If there is no good rule, check the spelling of the word in a dictionary each time you write, until you remember the correct spelling.

In addition, most languages have recurring spelling patterns. Find them out and apply them. In English, for instance, a consonant is often doubled before the progressive form **-ing**, e.g., **winning, occurring**. In French, **-e** appears at the end of many adjectives even though it is not pronounced, e.g., **mien**, "my" masculine, and **mienne**, "my" feminine. It is also important to learn how far one can apply the rule. For instance, in English, the consonant does not have to be doubled before the progressive form in **traveling**.

Avoid misspelling the same word over and over again. Most people find that they misspell the same words all the time. This can be avoided by making a list of such words to refer to or by developing a special mnemonic to help you remember the correct spelling. For instance, if you cannot remember whether **occurr** or **occured** is the correct spelling in the past tense, tell yourself that both consonants in this word are doubled before the ending **-ed**.

Use a spell-checker. Computer software with spell-checkers is available for a number of languages. Check with a language instructor, language lab, or software manufacturer.

PROBLEM 5
I never know how to punctuate in the foreign language.

Find out similarities and differences between your own and the foreign language. If you are studying a related language, many punctuation rules will turn out to be similar. For instance, all Indo-European languages put periods at the end of declarative sentences and question marks at the end of questions, although in Spanish an inverted question mark is placed at the beginning of a question as well. However, there may be some major differences between languages in the placement of other punctuation marks. For instance, in Russian, a comma is always placed before a dependent clause, but in English this is not necessarily the case. Compare the Russian **Ya znayu, kto on** with its English equivalent, **I know who he is.**

Learn the rules. In some languages, rules for punctuation are quite clear and unambiguous. For instance, in German all nouns are capitalized, but in English only certain nouns are written with a capital letter. If you are a speaker of English, where capitalizing is sometimes a matter of interpretation, you will find the German system quite rigid.

Find out how native speakers feel about punctuation. In some languages, such as Russian, punctuation is considered just as important as spelling, whereas in other languages, such as in English, there is more tolerance for imperfect punctuation. Hence, it is useful for a learner of Russian to spend some time learning how Russian punctuation works.

$\mathcal{A}$FTERWORD

By now you should have a much clearer understanding about yourself as a language learner, the language learning process, how to set realistic goals, and how to find an environment that will help you realize these goals. You should also have a better grasp of what you can do to help yourself become a more effective language learner: how to take charge of your learning, how to use what you know, how to assess the strategies you use, and how to improve your use of techniques in speaking, listening, reading, and writing.

Your success in learning a foreign language depends largely on how well you assess what you need to *do* at each stage of development. You should consider whether you will learn more by working in a classroom or by living abroad and using the language, and whether you should stress a particular skill.

You will need to assess what background knowledge about language and the world you already have and what you need to learn. At the same time, you will need to become aware of your learning strategies and of ways to improve them so that you learn more quickly and efficiently. You may also need to be conscious of the degree to which your feelings inhibit your learning and find ways to reduce their negative impact.

Remember that language learning can be a lifelong process and that your goals, knowledge, motivation, and strategies will vary, depending on your own situation and on your degree of language proficiency.

If you become actively involved in the process of learning, your chances of achieving your goals are immensely improved. Learning a foreign language is a complex undertaking, but if you know more about the process and about your own approach to the task, it can be a very rewarding, enriching, and enjoyable experience.

APPENDIX A

Addresses of Major Publishers of Foreign Language Materials

Althelstan
P.O. Box 8025
La Jolla, CA 92038-8025
(619) 689-1757
FAX: (619) 689-9270

Barron's Educational Series
250 Wireless Blvd.
Hauppauge, NY 11788
(516) 434-3311

D.C. Heath and Company
125 Spring Street
Lexington, MA 02173
1-800-334-3284

Delta Systems Co.
1400 Miller Parkway
McHenry, IL 60050-7030
(815) 363-3582
(800) 323-8270
FAX (815) 363-2948

EMC Publishing
300 York Ave.
St Paul, MN 55101
(612) 771-1555
(800) 328-1452
FAX (800) 328-4564

Films Incorporated
5547 N. Ravenswood Ave.
Chicago, IL 60640-1199
(312) 878-2600
(800) 323-4222
FAX (312) 868-0416

Gessler Publishing Company
55 West 13th St.
New York, NY 10011-7958
(212) 627-0099
FAX (212) 627-5948

Glencoe-Macmillan/
McGraw-Hill
936 Eastwind Drive
Westerville, OH 43081
(614) 899-4206
FAX (614) 899-4414

Harcourt Brace and
Company
7555 Caldwell Avenue
Chicago, IL 60648
(708) 647-8822
(800) 237-2665
FAX (708) 647-9424

Heinle & Heinle Publishers
20 Park Plaza
Boston, MA 02116-4501
(617) 451-1940
(800) 237-0053
FAX (617) 426-4379

Holt, Rinehart & Winston
1627 Woodland Ave.
Austin, TX 78741
(512) 440-5710

Houghton Mifflin Company
One Beacon St.
Boston, MA 02108
(617) 725-5835

John Wiley & Sons
605 Third Ave.
New York, NY 10158-0012
(212) 850-6000
FAX (212) 850-6088

Kendall/Hunt Publishing
Company
4050 Westmark Dr.
Dubuque, IA 52002
(319) 589-1000

Langenscheidt Publishers
46-35 54th Rd.
Maspeth, NY 11378
(718) 784-0055
(800) 432-6277
FAX (718) 784-0640

Longman Publishing Group
10 Bank St.
White Plains, NY 10606-1951
(914) 993-5000

McGraw Hill-College Division
1221 Avenue of the Americas
New York, NY 10020
(212) 512-2892
FAX (212) 512-6260

National Audio-Visual
Center
8700 Edgewood Dr.
Capitol Heights, MD 20743
(301) 763-1850

National Textbook Company
4255 W. Touhy Ave.
Lincolnwood, IL 60646
(708) 679-5500
(800) 323-4900
FAX (708) 679-2495

PICS—Project in International Communication Studies
270 International Center
University of Iowa
Iowa City, IA 52242-1802
(319) 335-2335

Prentice Hall College
Division
Route 9W
Englewood Cliffs, NJ 07632
(201) 592-2377

Rand McNally Educational
Publishing
8255 N. Central Park Ave.
Skokie, IL 60076
(708) 673-9100
(800) 678-7263
FAX (708) 673-1985

Scott, Foresman and
Company
1900 East Lake Ave.
Glenview, IL 60025
(708) 729-3000
FAX (708) 486-3660

Yale University Press
92A Yale Station
New Haven, CT 06520
(203) 432-0958
FAX (203) 432-2394

APPENDIX B

Addresses of Useful Organizations

American Council on the
Teaching of Foreign
Languages
6 Executive Plaza
Yonkers, N.Y. 10701
(914) 963-8830
FAX (914) 963-1275

CALICO
Duke University
Box 90267
Durham, NC 27708-0267
(919) 660-3180
FAX (919) 660-3183

Center for Applied
Linguistics
1118 22nd St., N.W.
Washington, DC 20037
(202) 429-9292

College Board
Programs/Educational
Testing Service
Rosedale Rd.
Princeton, NJ. 08541
(609) 734-5320

Council on International
Educational Exchange
205 East 42nd St.
New York, NY 10017
(212) 661-1414, ext. 1219

ERIC Clearinghouse on
Languages & Linguistics
1118 22nd St., N.W.
Washington, DC 20037
(202) 429-9292

French Cultural
Services/F.A.C.S.E.A/
Alliances Françaises
972 Fifth Ave.
New York, NY 10021
(212) 439-1458

Goethe House
1014 Fifth Ave.
New York, NY 10028
(212) 439-8700
FAX (212) 439-8705

Goethe Institute
1607 New Hampshire Ave. N.W.
Washington, DC 20009
(202) 319-0702

Instituto Cervantes
122 E. 42nd St.
Apt. 807
New York, NY 10168
(212) 689-4232

Inter-America Student
Programs
837 Glenwood Avenue N.
Minneapolis, MN 55405
(612) 377-1000

National Association of
Self-Instructional Language
Programs (NASILP)
John B. Means,
Executive Director
Critical Languages, 022-38
Temple University
Philadelphia, PA 19122
(215) 787-8268

National Registration
Center for Study Abroad
823 N. 2nd St.
P.O. Box 1393
Milwaukee, WI 43201
(414) 278-0631
FAX (414) 271-8884

Ohio State University
Foreign Language
Publications
34 Pressey Hall
1070 Carmack Rd.
Columbus, OH 43210-1002
(614) 292-3838

$\mathcal{A}$BOUT THE $\mathcal{A}$UTHORS

JOAN RUBIN (Ph.D., Yale) is an anthropologist and specialist in second language learning, listening comprehension, and language and technology. She has achieved near-native competence in several languages and is considered a "good language learner." Dr. Rubin has promoted "learning how to learn" a foreign language through research, writing, and workshops conducted at universities and government language agencies in many countries, including Australia, Italy, and Hong Kong. Dr. Rubin has been a professor at Georgetown University, the University of Hawaii, the University of North Carolina, and the University of California, Berkeley. As Senior Research Scholar, Department of Slavic Languages and Literatures, George Washington University, from 1990 to 1993, Dr. Rubin collaborated with Dr. Irene Thompson on research to enhance Russian listening comprehension. This research paralleled related research Dr. Rubin conducted on promoting Spanish listening comprehension by using video. Her volume, *Learner Strategies and Language Learning,* co-edited with A. Wenden, won the Mildenberger Prize of the Modern Language Association. Her interests in language and technology led Dr. Rubin to create the the Cindy Award-winning *Language Learning Strategies Disc,* which enables students to examine and develop their own language learning strategies. She has also produced a series of ten video lessons to teach effective English (as a second language) for the workplace. A pioneer in research on the learner strategies of "good language learners" and on sources of miscommunication across languages and cultures, Dr. Rubin's investigations have inspired major research in both areas.

IRENE THOMPSON (Ph.D., George Washington) is a psycholinguist and specialist in second language learning and teaching, language testing, and classroom methodology. In addition to being bilingual in Russian and English, Dr. Thompson is proficient in several other languages. She considers herself a "strategic" language learner. Dr. Thompson is a professor at George Washington University, where she chairs the Department of Slavic Languages. She has also directed the Russian program at the State Department's Foreign Service Institute and taught at Middlebury College, Bryn Mawr College, Cornell University, and the University of Hawaii. A veteran of over 25 years of practical language teaching, Dr. Thompson is active in many professional organizations, She has conducted workshops and seminars for high school and college teachers on curriculum design, classroom methodology, materials preparation, learner strategies, and language testing around the country. In 1990 she received the Florence Steiner Award from the American Council on the Teaching of Foreign Language for service to the profession. Along with many journal articles, she is co-author with Emily Urevich of a two-volume reader, *Reading Real Russian.*